MOOCs, High Technology, and Higher Learning

REFORMING HIGHER EDUCATION: Innovation and the Public Good

William G. Tierney and Laura W. Perna, Series Editors

MOOCs, HIGH TECHNOLOGY & HIGHER LEARNING

Robert A. Rhoads

Johns Hopkins University Press

BALTIMORE

© 2015 Johns Hopkins University Press
All rights reserved. Published 2015
Printed in the United States of America on acid-free paper
9 8 7 6 5 4 3 2 1

Johns Hopkins University Press
2715 North Charles Street
Baltimore, Maryland 21218-4363
www.press.jhu.edu

Library of Congress Cataloging-in-Publication Data

Rhoads, Robert A.
    MOOCs, high technology, and higher learning / Robert A. Rhoads.
    pages cm. — (Reforming higher education: innovation and the
public good)
    Includes bibliographical references and index.
    ISBN 978-1-4214-1779-0 (hardcover) — ISBN 978-1-4214-1780-6
(electronic) — ISBN 1-4214-1779-0 (hardcover) 1. MOOCs
(Web-based instruction) 2. Open learning. 3. Distance education.
4. Education, Higher—Computer-assisted instruction. 5. Education—
Effect of technological innovations on. I. Title.
    LB1044.87.R495 2015
    378.1'7344678—dc23   2014049508

A catalog record for this book is available from the British Library.

*Special discounts are available for bulk purchases of this book. For more
information, please contact Special Sales at 410-516-6936 or specialsales
@press.jhu.edu.*

Johns Hopkins University Press uses environmentally friendly book
materials, including recycled text paper that is composed of at least
30 percent post-consumer waste, whenever possible.

Contents

Acknowledgments

Special thanks to Laura Perna and Bill Tierney, series editors, for convincing me to undertake this project and for their superb feedback on early drafts. Also, I want to thank Greg Britton, Editorial Director at Johns Hopkins University Press, who has supported my work a number of times and who is always positive and encouraging. Thanks to all the JHUP staff who moved the book along. I also want to acknowledge research assistance from three of my doctoral students: Maria Sayil Camacho, Brit Toven-Lindsey, and Jennifer Berdan Lozano. Thanks to another of my doctoral students—Lauren Ilano—for her superb editing and work on the index. And finally, thanks from the bottom of my heart to Xiaoyang for standing by me even during those times when I get obsessed with completing a project such as this one.

MOOCs, High Technology, and Higher Learning

1

Introduction

The Rise of the MOOC

When the *New York Times* proclaimed 2012 "The Year of the MOOC," it wasn't as if there were no other stories that year. After all, the world survived the supposed end of the Mayan calendar, Mark Zuckerberg's Facebook going public on the New York Stock Exchange, and a euro in crisis. Natural disasters also struck, with typhoon Bopha hitting the Philippines and superstorm Sandy ravaging the East Coast of the United States. Other tragic news captured widespread attention, such as when an African American teenager, Trayvon Martin, was killed walking home from a local convenience store in Sanford, Florida. Mass shootings in Sandy Hook, Connecticut, and Aurora, Colorado, reminded most of us once again of a national sickness linked to violence and easy access to automatic weapons. There was positive news too. President Barack Obama, prior to his reelection, came out in support of gay marriage. The 2012 Summer Olympics in London was hailed as a rousing success; "Linsanity" captured the fascination of basketball fans around the world, especially Chinese and Chinese Americans who had a new NBA favorite in Jeremy Lin. With all that happened, 2012 could easily have been the Year of Pussy Riot, Aung San Suu Kyi, or Xi Jinping. But none of the headlines of 2012 could rival the revolutionary potential of the massive open online course, or MOOC (Pappano 2012).

The media certainly played a role in elevating the MOOC's popularity, evidencing an insatiable appetite at times, but the rapid rise and expansion of the movement made it hard to ignore. In December 2013, edSurge, an independent information resource community focusing on educational technology developments, reported that over 1,200 MOOCs had been offered since 2011 by more than two hundred universities involving some 10 million students. edSurge went on to point out that the MOOC movement had grown from approximately one hundred courses offered in 2012 to nearly seven hundred at the start of 2013 and that there were on average two new MOOCs created every day.[1] The data reported by edSurge may be on the conservative side, given that by October 2013 the *Wall Street Journal* reported that Coursera, a MOOC start-up company, had attracted over 5 million users and edX, a nonprofit partnership between the Massachusetts Institute of Technology and Harvard, had drawn 1.3 million (Fowler 2013). Given the dynamic and global quality of the movement, its zenith may still be in the distance. What is clear though from both the data and media coverage is that the popularity of MOOCs spread like a prairie fire, even beyond the imagination of the early MOOC innovators.

In a June 2013 talk delivered at the Faculty Center at the University of California, Los Angeles, I described the seemingly overnight explosion of MOOCs as "MOOC Madness." Similarly, Audrey Watters (2013b) dubbed the phenomenon "MOOC Mania" and Jeffrey Young (2013) "MOOC Hype" to capture the madness of it all—not "madness" in the sense of mental illness, but the madness of Christmas shopping on Black Friday or buying books at the campus bookstore on the first day of classes. MOOCs seemed to be virtually everywhere—literally! The revolution had come, and it was the MOOC. This is what we were led to believe by all the media coverage, right? Indeed, MOOCs were described as having the ability to "revolutionize how higher ed is delivered" (Selingo 2012), "change the world" (Carey 2012), take "online learning to the next level" (Lewin 2012b), offer "breakthrough delivery models" (Young 2012), and "transform higher education" (Kolowich 2013b). But it was hard to live up to such press, and MOOCs eventually faced blowback, a reality highlighted later in this book. In some sense, MOOCs have changed the world, or at least how we think about learning within the context of higher education. But they have perhaps not done so as profoundly as some had hoped—or not yet, anyway.

From MOOC Madness to blowback, the discourse surrounding MOOCs reveals their potential as both educational opportunity and as a challenge to dominant views of teaching and learning (Selwyn and Bulfin 2014). But what exactly is a MOOC? One of the major problems in answering this question is the vast diversity in MOOC offerings and the range of learner experiences they promote, a point highlighted in Jonathan Haber's 2014 book *MOOCs*, which chronicled his yearlong quest to complete the equivalency of an online bachelor's degree in philosophy, described as his Degree of Freedom. As Haber pointed out, some courses attempt to mimic the materials and requirements of a face-to-face university course, while others simply offer bits and pieces of a course.

A further complexity is that MOOCs are often conflated with more traditional notions of an online course or a hybrid course that combines elements of both face-to-face instruction and online materials. An example of this confusion was apparent in a 2013 *Chronicle of Higher Education* opinion piece in which Andrew Valls, an associate professor of political science at Oregon State University, asked "Who's Afraid of the Big Bad MOOC?," alluding to resistance to MOOCs on the part of faculty colleagues. The problem with this article was that, in his defense of MOOCs, Valls discussed how he made use of a variety of open course materials in his face-to-face teaching, essentially confusing hybrid courses with MOOCs. He seemed to miss the point that many MOOCs offer a complete course in and of themselves and that in some cases they are used to replace traditional face-to-face instruction; the latter point is, of course, a major source of faculty opposition. Few professors I know are opposed to borrowing online materials from other courses—including MOOCs—as part of creating a hybrid course or "flipping" the classroom, but many are reluctant to give up control of the curriculum by adopting MOOCs as substitutes for their own courses. It is not my intent here to be overly critical of Valls, as I believe he was actually on to something in noting the usefulness of MOOCs in combination with other instructional strategies, a point I return to in the final chapter when I discuss xsMOOC (MOOCs with extra support). Again, a good deal of the problem is a lack of shared understanding as to what constitutes a MOOC.

In 2012, EDUCAUSE, a nonprofit membership association supporting information technology to improve higher education, offered clarity about the nature of MOOCs when they issued an Executive Briefing titled, "What Campus Leaders Need to Know about MOOCs." Some key points include the following: MOOCs potentially target thousands of students at a time; most rely on traditional lecture approaches (typically digitally recorded); some encourage students to self-organize study or discussion groups (with most MOOCs offering little support for such self-organizing); some institutions seem to be experimenting with MOOCs as a brand extension, while others are trying to determine how MOOCs fit their instructional portfolio; MOOCs may catalyze new approaches to credentialing (indeed they have, with both for-profits and nonprofits offering a variety of credentials); and business models for achieving a return on investment are still evolving (although the original idea of the MOOC was not intended to generate revenue). Another point to consider is that MOOCs typically are offered in a synchronous format, meaning learners participate at the same pace, although in instances they may have asynchronous elements, wherein learners proceed at their own pace. The Executive Briefing went on to note, "MOOCs are online courses where lectures are typically 'canned,' quizzes and testing are automated, and student participation is voluntary. They attain large scale by reducing instructor contact with individual students; students often rely on self-organized study and discussion groups" (EDUCAUSE 2012, 1). This is one basic way to think about a MOOC that is helpful for now. Of course, as the phenomenon of the MOOC grew so did its complexity.

A Brief Sojourn

I first entered the world of the MOOC back in the fall of 2011, after returning from a sabbatical in China, where I had studied the cultural transformation of the Chinese research university. It was a sociological study, as is most of my work. I am not a scholar of high technology, computerization, adult or distance education, or instructional technology. Instead, I am a sociologist of education. I focus mainly on universities and university life, including academic culture, and primarily employ theories about education, social movements, and organizational change. My thinking tends to be grounded in the interdisciplinary school of thought typically described as critical theory. To put it another way, I am concerned about issues of inequality and the transformation of societies and educational organizations for the purpose of creating greater opportunities for disadvantaged populations. I particularly find the work of the Brazilian educational theorist Paulo Freire helpful in framing my research.

My vision of education is shaped by what I describe as a critical humanist perspective, often discussed in educational venues as critical pedagogy. Critical humanists believe that education ought to play a pivotal role in helping students unmask the ways in which forms of power and domination operate to shape their interactions with the worlds they inhabit. This version of education aims to free one's consciousness from a variety of constraints, typically informed and shaped by the interests of powerful classes and groups of people. Freire (1970), in his classic work *Pedagogy of the Oppressed*, described this process of liberation as *conscientization*—a Portuguese term often translated as "critical consciousness."

For Freire, democratic dialogues are at the heart of empowering forms of education, for it is only through a deep questioning of the world and the ways in which power and domination are manifested that one ultimately achieves critical understanding. Cornel West (1993) offered insight here: "Freire's project of democratic dialogue is attuned to the concrete operations of power (in and out of the classroom) and grounded in the painful yet empowering process of *conscientization*. This process embraces a critical demystifying moment in which structures of domination are laid bare and political engagement is imperative" (xiii).

Education from a Freirian perspective is not so much about conveying knowledge in a one-directional manner to students but instead involves facilitating deep dialogues in which students actively engage in the process of knowledge critique and construction. An idealized outcome is that students become agents in shaping their own histories. Again, West is helpful: "This unique fusion of social theory, moral outrage and political praxis constitutes a kind of pedagogical politics of conversion in which objects of history constitute themselves as active subjects of history ready to make a fundamental difference in the quality of the lives they individually and collectively live" (xiii). West calls attention to the importance of praxis (akin to agency) in Freire's thinking and the role of education in helping students come to terms with their lives not as victims of history but as subjects of it. This version of education is much more than mastering skill sets through drills but instead involves something significantly deeper—the emancipation of one's consciousness. Hence, a belief in the power of Freirian pedagogy frames my analysis of MOOCs and the overall MOOC movement. A key part of such analysis is recognizing the importance that social movements play in advancing educational reform.

I tend to see the most important transformations in education taking place within the context of complex and expansive social movements, having previously spelled out this perspective in detail while addressing a variety of cases (Rhoads 1998, 2003; Rhoads and Liu 2009; Rhoads and Mina 2001; Rhoads and Rhoades 2005; Slocum and Rhoads 2009). The key point is that when I write about MOOCs, I do so as a critical sociologist interested in understanding their impact for higher education and society, particularly in terms of how the MOOC movement intersects with issues of power and social inequality. I recognize MOOCs as being closely tied to the powerful cultural influence of high technology, including the expanding role of the Internet and Internet-related applications. Although I see MOOCs arising largely from the influence of high-tech culture, at the same time MOOCs constitute a unique and somewhat independent force having significant implications for society and how we think about higher learning.

I see MOOCs as constituting a social movement on the basis that multiple social actors and organizations have aligned their actions to such an extent that the phenomenon takes on the classic characteristics of a loosely coordinated activity with common lines of action and similar definitions of the situation (Blumer 1990). As a complex and loosely coupled assemblage, the MOOC movement evidences a variety of tensions and uncertainties, including little agreement about where the movement may actually be heading. The tensions and uncertainties present a major challenge to analyzing the MOOC movement at a particular point in its history and necessitate great clarity in advancing a meaningful argument. Accordingly, I offer seven theses that frame the analysis presented in this book.

Seven Key Theses

Thesis 1: MOOCs may be understood as an outgrowth of the open educational resource (OER) and open courseware (OCW) movements, evidencing to a great extent some of the same values of openness. This thesis is primarily discussed in this first chapter as part of my effort to contextualize the rise of MOOCs. Of course, the development of the World Wide Web and the Internet made the OER and OCW movements possible and thus also warrants modest treatment. Furthermore, economic and cultural conditions, including most notably the Great Recession as well as growing support for online education, also helped support the rise of MOOCs.

Thesis 2: The MOOC movement is supported by a complex array of social actors and organizations, which in essence constitute an organizational system. This system represents the convergence of both private and public good interests that at different points in time may be either complementary or contradictory. This thesis forms the thrust of chapter 2.

Thesis 3: MOOCs must be differentiated into cMOOCs and xMOOCs, with the former based primarily on connectivist learning theory and requiring high levels of self-directed behavior and the latter being a more institutionalized version of the MOOC dependent to a greater extent on well-defined course objectives and structure. The distinction between cMOOCs and xMOOCs and the relevance of connectivist learning theory will be discussed extensively in chapter 3.

Thesis 4: xMOOCs dominate the MOOC landscape (in part because of challenges tied to implementing cMOOCs), but there are critical problems that must be addressed when considering scaling xMOOCs to expand college access. Most notably, xMOOCs targeting remedial and lower-division students in a massive way are likely to require additional support structures to promote meaningful student success. This is one of the most critical arguments contained in this book, and it will be discussed at different points, including in chapter 3 as part of differentiating cMOOCs and xMOOCs and in chapter 4 relative to a discussion of what I term "the problem of epistemology" and "the problem of pedagogy."

Thesis 5: Elite universities dominate the MOOC landscape, which poses a set of unique problems and challenges for the overall MOOC movement and for higher education more generally. I reference this thesis in several places but specifically highlight this and related issues in chapter 4 when I discuss "the problem of hegemony."

Thesis 6: Despite the growing importance diversity plays in higher education policy and practice worldwide, diversity and related issues are largely absent from policies, practices, and discussions relative to MOOCs. This is a key concern of chapter 4, and I describe it as "the problem of diversity."

Thesis 7: The MOOC movement has significant implications for faculty life, including the potential to refashion the nature of faculty work for certain segments of the professorate. This thesis is primarily discussed in chapter 4 relative to what I describe as "the problem of faculty labor," but it also is raised elsewhere, including in chapter 5 as part of a discussion of intellectual property concerns.

The preceding seven theses capture the thrust of my argument, but of course other minor assertions are offered here and there, typically serving to advance one of the aforementioned key theses. The overall argument is not a simple linear one, given that the issues are complex and the terrain of the MOOC ever changing. The movement is a young one, and it is difficult for anyone to envision what it will resemble three, four, or five years down the road. A complex and dynamic phenomenon necessitates sophisticated treatment. Accordingly, I ask readers to exercise a certain degree of patience in allowing ideas and arguments to unfold as the narrative moves forward.

Writing in the innovative online journal *Hybrid Pedagogy*, Jesse Stommell (2012) argued, "Too many people are drinking the MOOC Kool-aid (or dumping it out hastily) when what we need to do is look closely at the Kool-aid to see what we can learn from it." This pretty much sums up my goal in this book. Accordingly, I begin by contextualizing the rise of the MOOC movement (mostly addressing thesis 1), including a discussion of key factors that shaped the emergence and expansion of MOOCs. The following are central to the remainder of the chapter: (1) advances associated with Web 2.0 and concomitantly changes in a variety of information and communication technologies, contributing to the emergence of highly popular social media sites such as Myspace, Facebook, Twitter, and YouTube; (2) the rise of an Internet-based knowledge commons and with it the emergence of the OER and OCW movements; (3) an economic crisis that resulted in funding reductions for colleges and universities, expanded calls for enhanced faculty productivity, and demands for improved and more efficient service to students as customers; and (4) calls for expanding online education.

Technological Advances and the World Wide Web

Complex social phenomena rarely have a clear beginning or ending. We simply force such finality onto them as part of making sense of the human experience. History is written in thematic episodes, told in broad narrative strokes, but it is not lived that way. Despite the randomness of beginnings and endings, I select changes of the 1990s involving technological updates to the World Wide Web as a starting point. The changes led to what is typically described as Web 2.0 and played a pivotal role in the eventual rise of MOOCs. I could obviously go back even further, perhaps to the invention of transistors and then the integrated circuit (IC), or microchip. I could highlight the work of computer scientists such as Jack Kilby of Texas Instruments and William Shockley of Bell Labs, whose ideas helped to usher in the age of computerization, where PCs, Macs, and iPhones became essential devices. But others far more technologically qualified than myself have traced that trajectory of innovation along with related social and cultural developments. Included among such narratives is Martin Kenney's edited volume *Understanding Silicon Valley: The Anatomy of an Entrepreneurial Region* (2000) and AnnaLee Saxenian's *Regional Advantage: Culture and Competition in Silicon Valley and Route 128* (1996).

Web 2.0 represents a steady stream of advances in Web technologies taking place over a relatively short period of time, mostly during the 1990s (Cormode and Krishnamurthy 2008). There is no definitive difference between the early World Wide Web, often termed Web 1.0, and the present-day Web 2.0. Instead, the divide separating these versions of the Web is encapsulated by an accumulation of changes adding greater interactive capacity, more dynamic graphics and visualizations, and enhanced hardware and software, all of which dramatically increased interactivity and connectivity, ultimately rendering the social media of today commonplace. Seen in this light, the term "Web 2.0" is "used largely metaphorically to suggest a major software upgrade" (Tredinnick 2006, 229). Perhaps "upgrade" is an understatement, as the changes arguably were quite transformative. Richard Baraniuk (2008) captured aspects of the transformation: "Web 2.0—Remix, which emerged around 2001, emphasizes participation and interaction. . . . Using tools such as XML [Extensible Markup Language], wikis, tagging, and social networking, the results have included exponentially growing community Web sites like Myspace, the user-generated encyclopedia Wikipedia, hundreds of millions of user-generated YouTube videos, tens of millions of blogs, distributed file-sharing projects like Napster and BitTorrent" (241). Web 2.0 thus was an enhancement largely in terms of social learning and connectivity. Can Web 3.0 be far away? And what will be its defining difference? The answer may already be emerging with the definitive quality of Web 3.0 technologies likely to be tied to artificial intelligence (AI) and the potential to facilitate Web adaptation to meet the needs of users. Again, Baraniuk is helpful:

> Web 3.0—Semantic Web, which is currently emerging, will add intelligence via natural language processing, data-mining, machine learning, and other artificial intelligence technologies. . . . The Web 3.0 will be attentive to and even predict user needs and behavior to provide richer and more meaningful and useful interactions. As such, it holds much promise for OE [open education]. OE 3.0 projects will not just develop and deliver open content to students; they will also monitor student interactions with it, analyze those interactions, and then send rich feedback not only to the students about their learning, but also to the communities of curriculum builders, authors, and instructors to drive iterative improvement of the learning materials. (242)

Baraniuk offered interesting points to consider as the world of online education continues to expand with more sophisticated pedagogical options becoming available. MOOCs too will no doubt benefit from such advances.

Darcy DiNucci often is credited with being the first to use the term "Web 2.0." Writing in 1999, she sought to capture the changing times: "What we need to remember, though, is that the Web, as we know it now, is a fleeting thing. . . . The relationship of Web 1.0 to the Web of tomorrow is roughly the equivalent of Pong to *The Matrix*. . . . The Web will be understood not as screenfuls of text and graphics but as a transport mechanism, the ether through which interactivity happens" (38). Along similar lines, Web 1.0 has been described as "the static" Web and 2.0 as the more "dynamic" Web, more useful in "creating, developing and using applications over the Internet" (Cervinschi and Butucea 2010, 39).

A key facet then separating Web 1.0 from 2.0 is the idea of collective intelligence, also discussed in terms of crowdsourcing. Tim O'Reilly and John Battelle (2009) published a well-known white paper about the importance of this form of online collaboration made possible by technological enhancements to the Web. As they explained,

> To understand where the Web is going, it helps to return to one of the fundamental ideas underlying Web 2.0, namely that successful network applications are systems for harnessing collective intelligence. Many people now understand this idea in the sense of "crowdsourcing," meaning that a large group of people can create a collective work whose value far exceeds that provided by any of the individual participants. The Web as a whole is a marvel of crowdsourcing, as are marketplaces such as those on eBay and craigslist, mixed media collections such as YouTube and Flickr, and the vast personal lifestream collections on Twitter, MySpace, and Facebook. (2)

O'Reilly and Battelle also noted that with these transformations in technologies, the Web 2.0 "was on its way to becoming a robust platform for a culture-changing generation of computer applications and services" (1). Given the changes in how a wide range of folks today communicate and remain connected to one another as well as make new social connections through the benefits of 2.0 technologies, describing these developments as "culture-changing" certainly is apropos.

The capacity for collective intelligence lends itself to groups of Web users working together creatively to coconstruct ideas, software, and applications, typically without a clear sense of individual ownership. This version of the Web "is presented as a process of ceding control over applications to users, enabling users to extract information and data and reuse that information and data in a flexible way . . . even to change the structure of the information system itself" (Tredinnick 2006, 229). This collective quality of Web 2.0 and its capacity for collaborative work is in part why some have described the Internet as democratizing knowledge and information. John Seely Brown and Richard Adler (2008) discussed Web 2.0 changes and their relevance to new ways of thinking and working:

The latest evolution of the Internet, the so-called Web 2.0, has blurred the line between producers and consumers of content and has shifted attention from access to information toward access to other people. New kinds of online resources—such as social networking sites, blogs, wikis, and virtual communities—have allowed people with common interests to meet, share ideas, and collaborate in innovative ways. Indeed, the Web 2.0 is creating a new kind of participatory medium that is ideal for supporting multiple modes of learning. (18)

This new participatory medium—in essence a "knowledge commons"—is at the heart of the open educational resource (OER) and open courseware (OCW) movements.

The Knowledge Commons and the OER/OCW Movements

The open educational resource movement emerged in the context of Web 1.0 but was reformulated in more social and engaging ways as a result of Web 2.0 advances. Particularly, opportunities linked to collective intelligence and inter-activity raised new challenges about how knowledge and information might be shared and produced by co-users. This necessitated that Web users/producers consider new ways of thinking about ownership of knowledge and information, resulting in the introduction of ideals associated with an information or knowl-edge commons (Brown 2008).

The knowledge commons is a complex idea with its roots reaching back to debates about private land ownership versus the notion of a commons (shared conceptions of land usage); the ideal of a commons flourished in parts of Eu-rope until the late 1800s, when it was largely challenged by the expansion of capitalism and industrialization (in the form of the Industrial Revolution). More recently, the ideal of the commons arose with regard to debates about environmental degradation and issues of sustainability. From the perspective of a commons, global ecology ought to concern all of us, as we all share in the earth's stewardship and any hope of securing a sustainable future. However, not everyone supports the logic of the commons; opponents often turn to biologist Garrett Hardin's "The Tragedy of the Commons" (1968) as a counterexample. Hardin described a scenario in which herdsmen hypothetically shared a common pasture only to destroy the land by putting too many cattle out to graze, each looking out for his own interest while ignoring the broader interest of the group as well as the ecology of the pasture. As Hardin argued, "Ruin is the distinction toward which all men rush, each pursuing his own best interest in a society that believes in the freedom of the commons. Freedom in a commons brings ruin to all" (1244).

Charlotte Hess and Elinor Ostrom, in the introduction to their edited book *Understanding Knowledge as a Commons* (2007), challenged Hardin's point of view, noting that commons scholars repeatedly found him to be mistaken on a number of points: "He was actually discussing open access rather than managed commons; he assumed little or no communication; he postulated that people act only in their immediate self-interest (rather than assuming that some individuals take joint benefits into account, at least to some extent); he offered only two solutions to correct the tragedy—privatization or government intervention" (11). As Hess and Ostrom went on to argue, numerous studies of shared natural resources demonstrate the ability of people to work together:

> Whether studying California ground water basins, North Atlantic fisheries, African community forests, or Nepalese irrigation systems, scientific case studies frequently seem to answer: *Au contraire, Monsieur Hardin!* There may be situations where this model can be applied, but many groups can effectively manage and sustain common resources if they have suitable conditions, such as appropriate rules, good conflict-resolution mechanisms, and well-defined group boundaries. (11)

The lesson to be taken from this, in terms of a Web-based knowledge commons, is that users can work together in a manner beneficial to the vast majority by creating appropriate rules and suitable mechanisms and boundaries to guide group norms. Indeed, a guiding structure for a Web-based knowledge commons has emerged in the form of open licensing.

Open licensing offers basic principles and norms for how ideas as products may be openly available on the Internet to a wide range of users. Knowledge commons advocates believe that the ideas are likely to be enhanced over time as more and more users produce revised content. Essentially, in the world of shared educational resources, users are just as likely to become producers.[2] Along these lines, Ahrash Bissell (2009) discussed the OER movement and some of the related ideals of shared knowledge:

> The open education movement is motivated by several shared beliefs that unite the community. First, knowledge can and should be free. This holds true not just in the economic sense, but also in the sense that knowledge should be able to evolve and adapt as things change and in reflection of local needs and cultures.

Second, most educators and others who engage with OER do so because they desire to improve educational systems and opportunities for learning. Teaching and learning should be creative acts, free of unnecessary legal constraint in our collective efforts to enable educational attainment worldwide. Third . . . the lines that traditionally divided content producers from content users are blurring. Basically, everyone is either a creator or a consumer some of the time. (98)

What we see here is the elevation of teaching and learning over the ownership of intellectual property, the opportunity to educate or be educated taking precedence over the opportunity to profit. This is quite revolutionary. However, such ideals are not necessarily embraced by everyone using Internet technologies to produce or create ideas and products.

There is another facet to the open access argument in the form of what John Willinsky called "the access principle," articulated in his 2006 book by the same name. Although Willinsky focused on scientific research, the basic principle he advanced also informs the knowledge commons idea. For Willinsky, access is a matter of public obligation. As he wrote, "A commitment to the value and quality of research carries with it a responsibility to extend the circulation of such work as far as possible and ideally to all who are interested in it and all who might profit by it" (xii). The same may be said of ideas, software, and even university courses, if in fact one believes in their value. Hence, a good deal of effort in recent years has gone into developing licenses so that products and ideas might be more readily shared.

There are numerous types of shared licenses and companies offering them, but a leader in this area is Creative Commons (CC), which offers a range of licenses varying significantly in terms of the degrees of freedom or openness applied to a particular work. CC was founded on the basic principle that Internet users desire to share their work as well as embrace the opportunity to reuse, modify, and redistribute the work and products of others in open and free-sharing spaces. As Bissell explained, "When a CC license is applied, permission has already been given, eliminating guesswork and uncertainty as to the expectations of the copyright holder. CC licenses have easy-to-read deeds, making it possible for non-lawyers to interpret the permissions that have been granted" (2009, 100). There are six basic options for CC licenses, all explained on their website, ranging from "Attribution," which provides the greatest freedom in terms of allowing a user to remix, tweak, or distribute a work (including for commercial purposes), to "Attribution-NonCommercial-NoDerivs," the most restrictive of the CC licenses, allowing users only to download and share a work with proper credit to the creator (users cannot change the original work in any way or use it commercially).[3] Choices offered by CC licenses provide basic guidelines to a Web-based knowledge commons and address some of the concerns generally expressed by commons scholars. Constructing easy-to-follow and easy-to-adopt guides enables effective cooperation and collaboration, thus encouraging application of the sort of collective intelligence made possible by Web 2.0 technologies.

The knowledge commons is in part a reaction to modern society and the increasingly legalized enclosure and privatization of the world's resources, including historically land, water, and minerals and more recently ideas. One of the major arenas that helped to propel the knowledge commons is the development of open source software (OSS). The typical model of innovation dominant in the United States and most advanced nations is the profit-ownership model with intellectual property protections. The idea is to offer protections to private inventors and creators so they might maximize the returns of their investment of time, energy, and creativity. This relatively common and widely accepted model of ownership was described as the "private investment" model by Eric von Hippel and Georg von Krogh (2003). Of particular importance, they contrasted the private investment model with the more recent "collective action" model, which operates on the basis of advantages associated with individuals working together to solve complex technical problems, with each having the opportunity to address her or his self-interest but at the same time assisting others. In this light, the outcomes—in the case of the Internet, perhaps alterations to applications and software—are seen as a public good and part of the knowledge commons. As von Hippel and von Krogh went on to note, this is more or less the model upon which OSS operates, although they also offered a new framework for furthering OSS development, combining elements of both the private investment and collective action models in the form of a "private-collective" model. The key point here is that users/producers engaged in the development of OSS helped to chart new ground with regard to the ownership of ideas and the relevance of collective intelligence.

A particular form of open source software—open source Learning Management Systems (LMS)—has been critical to expanding OER, specifically in terms of making the management of course materials easier while increasing accessibility for users. Examples of open source LMS include Dokeos, eFront, .LRN (Learn, Research, Network), Moodle (Modular Object-Oriented

Dynamic Learning Environment), and Sakai. Of course, the development of open source LMS was critical to the emergence of the open courseware (OCW) movement and eventually MOOCs.

As the OER movement expanded in reach, it was hardly surprising that academic materials associated with a college or university course eventually were included as resources openly available to online users. The emergence of the OCW movement then may be understood as an extension or outgrowth of OER. Such a perspective is consistent with definitions of OER, wherein the range of materials to be available go far beyond course materials and include such digitized items as software, papers, monographs, animations, simulations, games, and so forth (Downes 2007). Consistent with the ideals of the knowledge commons, making course materials available to teachers and learners around the world was seen as an idealized vision of higher education stressing access. In this sense, the OCW movement aligns well with Article 26 of the United Nations Universal Declaration of Human Rights, maintaining that "everyone has the right to education" and "higher education shall be equally accessible to all on the basis of merit" (Huijser, Bedford, and Bull 2008). Bissell explained it quite succinctly: "Knowledge can and should be free" (2009, 98).

Proposed as a concept around 2001, the OCW movement was to expand more rapidly than most could have predicted. By April of 2008, in anticipation of a meeting of the OpenCourseWare Consortium, two hundred member universities conducted an inventory of their total courses available and traffic to OCW sites. As Steve Carson (2009) pointed out, "Course materials from more than 6,200 courses were freely and openly available" with incomplete data revealing "more than 2.25 million visits were paid to those materials each month" (23). Carson went on to capture the historic significance of it all: "Only five and a half years before that meeting, not a single course had been shared via OCW, and the idea had only just been suggested by a group of faculty at Massachusetts Institute of Technology." Carson maintained that the very idea of universities making their course materials available for free on the Web "was unimaginable at the time the concept was first proposed in 2001 [and] . . . antithetical to the thinking of most universities at the time" (23).

MIT was the institutional leader in the OCW movement and at the forefront in establishing the OCW Consortium. Early on, MIT sought to make all its course syllabi available. The key role of the university in furthering the OCW movement was captured in a provocative 2008 article, "Minds on Fire," by John Seely Brown and Richard Adler. The article also conveyed key organizational facets to the growing OCW movement:

> The movement began in 2001 when the William and Flora Hewlett and the Andrew W. Mellon foundations jointly funded MIT's OpenCourseWare (OCW) initiative, which today provides open access to undergraduate- and graduate-level materials and modules from more than 1,700 courses (covering virtually all of MIT's curriculum). MIT's initiative has inspired hundreds of other colleges and universities in the United States and abroad to join the movement and contribute their own open educational resources. (18)

MIT went on to partner with Harvard University to form edX, a nonprofit organization designed to advance the engagement of both universities in online education, including OCW and eventually MOOCs. Following the lead of MIT and Harvard, other colleges and universities jumped on board the OCW train, with a variety of for-profit companies such as Coursera and Udacity forming as well (in some cases providing more advanced course platforms for universities).

The early OCW movement offered both the democratization of higher education as a public good as well as opportunities for entrepreneurialism and profit taking. Initially, it seemed everyone wanted either to further democratize college access or to develop revenue-generating models capable of tapping into the rapidly expanding global demand for higher education. In terms of profitability, entrepreneurs discussed offering course materials using an iTunes model, for instance, in which a very small fee might be charged to individual users per course. Others saw potential revenue flowing to companies offering support materials, such as required or recommended textbooks. Still others foresaw students potentially earning credit by completing open courses online and then purchasing a certificate after presumably verifying a basic level of course mastery. The thinking at the time was that although MIT and Harvard deferred from granting course credit, which could potentially compromise their brand, other institutions with less to lose might be willing to do so. Colorado State University, for example, emerged as one of the first universities to offer credit for the completion of open online courses including MOOCs (Lewin 2012a). Additionally, Pearson VUE testing eventually teamed with Udacity and edX to offer proctored tests as a way of verifying content mastery. Charging a fee for such tests was one more source of revenue, as was offering a certificate of completion, a policy adopted early on by Udacity and edX (Anderson

2013). The complexity of the organizational system that emerged to undergird both the OCW movement and the expansion of MOOCs was vast. In chapter 2, I specifically focus on the organizational and movement dynamics of the rise and expansion of OCW and MOOCs, but here it is worth highlighting the early values undergirding this historic educational turn.

The democratization of higher education in the form of expanding access to university courses for students and teachers was central to the early university-based OCW advocates. This was evident in MIT OCW, captured to some extent by its mission: "to provide free access to virtually all MIT course materials for educators, students and individual learners around the world. To extend the reach and impact of MIT OpenCourseWare and the OpenCourseWare concept" (Carson 2009, 26). MIT was essentially staking a claim to both digital and global preeminence and doing so while rejecting the dominant ethos of the day—marketization of university commodities, or what Sheila Slaughter and Gary Rhoades (2004) described as "academic capitalism." Carson explained it this way: "In proposing OCW at a time when the prevailing trends in higher education were toward commercialisation and competition, MIT also staked out a new model for the role of universities in the digital environment, one that reflected longstanding commitments in academia to dissemination of knowledge and shared scholarship—a model that would ultimately resonate worldwide" (25).

Skeptics questioned whether MIT and Harvard were truly about democratizing knowledge for the benefit of the world (consistent with a public good ideal), with more than a few offering an alternative possibility: The two academic giants were simply anticipating the growing dominance of globalized higher education markets and thus were further securing their global brand (Rhoads, Li, and Ilano 2015). Skeptics also emerged from among the faculty at the leading OCW/MOOC providers. For example, in May 2013 Harvard faculty sent a letter of concern to Michael Smith, dean of the Faculty of Arts and Sciences, not only raising questions about possible risks for the university but also expressing concerns about the potential damage to "the higher education system as a whole" (Jaschik 2013). Similar sorts of concerns arose at many campuses around the country, including most notably at San Jose State University (I say much more about this case later in the book), but also at such institutions as Amherst College and Duke University.

Although opposition arose among faculty toward various OCW initiatives, particularly with regard to the adoption of MOOCs and especially in cases where MOOCs appeared to be forced on academic programs without adequate faculty consultation, the reality was that higher education in the early twenty-first century exhibited a growing openness to online education. This shifting social context was critical to the overall growth of OCW and MOOCs.

Growing Support for Online Education

The for-profit higher education industry embraced online education as a strategy for expanding access to education early on, with nonprofits somewhat lagging behind. But by the late 1990s and early 2000s the tide began to shift, with more and more nonprofit colleges and universities pursuing online education options (I. E. Allen and Seaman 2007; Lytle 2011). Increased openness to online education was evident among a variety of key players involved in shaping nonprofit higher education, including policy makers, governing boards, and institutional leaders; certain segments of the professorate also were supportive, although it is safe to say that the majority remained highly skeptical.

An excellent institutional example of the increased vitality of online education is captured by the rise of Western Governors University. Based in Salt Lake City and founded in 1997, WGU was the brainchild of a group of nineteen United States governors, members of the Western Governors Association. The institution's motto says a good deal about its priorities: "Online. Accelerated. Affordable. Accredited." With the stress on online and competency-based learning, WGU played a pivotal role in helping to legitimize online education, paving the way in some sense for other nonprofit institutions to give more serious consideration to online teaching and learning strategies.

More recently, several state-level legislative bodies and governing boards challenged their respective states' public colleges and universities to make greater use of online education as both a cost-saving strategy and a method for expanding access. For example, the Council of Presidents of Arizona's Board of Regents released a September 2010 report, "The Arizona Higher Education Enterprise: Strategic Realignment 2010 Forward," calling for the three public universities—Arizona State, Northern Arizona, and the University of Arizona—to expand "access to baccalaureate degrees through the establishment of new baccalaureate degree campuses, expanded community college access and expanded online access" (21). Similarly, Florida's Board of Governors (2013), in a key report of the Task Force on Postsecondary Online Education, took action to create a "separate arm" of the state's public university system "to provide online degree programs" (1). The report went on to note, "The selected university will create an innovation and research center to ensure the state is a leader in the development of cutting-edge technology and instructional design for online programs and conduct research to help strengthen online degree programs and the success of online students" (1). In the summer of 2013, the California State Senate initially passed what was called the Online Education Bill, or SB 520, essentially aiming to require the state's public colleges and universities to offer credit for online courses such as MOOCs. Although the bill later stalled, the fact that it got as far as it did in California was further evidence that online education had arrived.

Political support for increased online postsecondary education was also evident among national leaders. For example, a December 2013 report issued by President Obama's Council of Advisors on Science and Technology (PCAST) reinforced the relevance of online teaching and learning. Although the report focused mostly on MOOCs, including their potential to transform higher education, the council also addressed online education in general, offering the following: The U.S. Department of Education should encourage regional accrediting bodies to be more flexible in considering that standards expected of an accredited degree may need to be modified relative to online courses and programs. The PCAST report also encouraged the federal government to further support competitive extramural grant programs for research and development in the area of online teaching and learning. President Obama emerged as a major advocate for online education, noting in an August 2013 speech at SUNY Buffalo that colleges and universities need "to embrace innovative new ways to prepare our students for a 21st-century economy and maintain a high level of quality without breaking the bank" (O'Neil 2013). He went on to praise the online master's program in computer science introduced earlier in the year by Georgia Institute of Technology.

Greater support for innovative forms of online teaching and learning also arose among leading philanthropic organizations. Key foundation leaders such as Jamie Merisotis of Lumina and Bill Gates of the Bill and Melinda Gates Foundation were major advocates of online education, seeing Internet-based educational solutions as vehicles to better prepare young adults for the demands of the twenty-first century. Sometimes they spoke in code, such as when Merisotis urged higher education leaders to "focus on such issues as increasing innovation to deliver more high-quality learning to larger numbers of students" (DiSalvio 2013). Gates often was more matter-of-fact, making online education one of the principal topics of his 2010 Annual Letter, noting that his foundation "is just at the start" of work in this arena, and adding, "a lot of people, including me, think this is the next place where the Internet will surprise people in how it can improve things."

Governmental and foundation leaders do not a trend make. But if there was any doubt that online education was to be a major force in the early decades of the twenty-first century, news story after news story by the *Chronicle of Higher Education* and the *New York Times*, among other print outlets, erased such doubts. For example, searching these two venues using the term "online education" (in August 2014) yielded 10,028 and 139,000 hits for the *Chronicle* and *Times* respectively ("online learning" yielded 6,881 and 39,800, respectively). By 2000, both newspapers were giving serious treatment to online education. Indeed, the *Chronicle* turned online education into everyday parlance through headlines such as these (all from May 2000):

- "Citing Benefits, 2 More States Plan Virtual Universities" (May 3)
- "Jesuit Colleges Try to Bring Their Values to Online Education" (May 8)
- "Congressman Worries Aloud: Is Online Education Any Good?" (May 10)
- "Duke U. Policy Sets Rules for Online-Course Ownership and Conflicts of Interest" (May 23)
- "A Deal Will Help Columbia U. Put Continuing-Education Courses Online" (May 24)

The *New York Times* was just as turned on and tuned in, with the following more recent headlines offering only a glimpse into the growing presence of online education:

- "Universities Team with Online Course Provider" (May 30, 2013)
- "Online Classes Move Closer to Degree Programs" (September 17, 2013)
- "European Universities Catch the Online Wave" (September 22, 2013)
- "Free Online University Receives Accreditation" (February 13, 2014)

The headlines often were eye-catching, but none came close to this one from the *New York Times:* "Snow Day? That's Great. Now Log In. Get to Class" (February 13, 2014). It seemed online education had the potential to even transform the cherished snow day.

A 2013 report sponsored by the Chronicle of Higher Education Inc., underwritten by Adobe Systems Inc. and Pearson, offered insight into the thinking of faculty and university presidents with regard to the potential of online education (Selingo 2013). For example, 60 percent of faculty and 79 percent of presidents surveyed saw hybrid courses employing both face-to-face and online components as having the potential to impact higher education positively. Generally speaking, most faculty and presidents were optimistic about the potential of blended and adaptive learning, as well as the use of interactive technologies, but they were more skeptical of competency-based degrees as well as the potential of MOOCs to positively impact higher education.

What all of this is meant to suggest is that a variety of key actors involved in supporting the higher education enterprise increasingly were open to expanding online education or at the very least incorporating online materials (typically digitized) into more traditional face-to-face courses. Here, though, it is important to recognize that online education was not always discussed in the same terms; some supporters of online education talked about the importance of building on face-to-face courses by incorporating blended or flipped classroom modalities, while other proponents went all in, arguing for the development of online courses and programs that might lead to college credits and possibly degrees, as in the cases of Western Governors University, University of the People, and the Florida Board of Governors. Of course, the "revolutionary" and "transformative" MOOCs eventually became the centerpiece of such discussions. MOOCs, as one manifestation of online education, seemed to hold the potential to save colleges and universities money, and in this regard they were particularly appealing. This is not surprising when one considers that the growing appeal of MOOCs coincided with a global economic crisis and reduced funding for colleges and universities in general. With difficult financial times came calls for greater accountability and doing more with less, including demands for increased faculty productivity.

The Economic Crisis and Higher Education

If technological enhancements in the form of Web 2.0 and the rise of the OCW movement were not enough to convince key players of the relevance of online education, the Great Recession of 2008 served to add propellant to the cause.[4] The recession, as most experts argued, was the outcome of the collapse of the U.S. housing bubble, which quickly mutated into a global epidemic, the "result of American contagion" (Landler 2008). State coffers took a heavy hit, leading many legislative bodies and governors to dramatically cut support for public higher education. For example, California's public universities saw massive cuts during the 2009–10 fiscal year: the University of California saw its budget cut $813 million, the California State University system was cut $625 million, and the California Community Colleges were cut $812 million. The consequences were grave for students. The UC Board of Regents approved fee increases of 15 percent for spring 2010 and another 15 percent for the subsequent fall semester (Newall 2009). In the face of such a dramatic financial crises, and with states struggling to generate adequate tax revenues, concerns about spending and issues of accountability took on heightened importance.

Besieged by revenue problems, state legislatures and governing bodies turned an even more critical eye to their public colleges and universities. Criticism ranged far and wide, including questions about student learning, low graduation rates, excessive institutional spending on frills, administrative bloat, meaningless faculty research, and faculty workload overall.[5] Chad Adelman and Kevin Carey, writing in 2009 for the Educator Sector policy think tank based on funding from the Lumina Foundation, offered support for some of the criticism:

> States need strong higher education systems, now more than ever. In the tumultuous, highly competitive 21st century economy, citizens and workers need knowledge, skills, and credentials in order to prosper. Yet many colleges and universities are falling short. Only about half of all entering freshmen complete a bachelor's degree in six years or less, and the numbers for black, Hispanic, and low-income students are even worse. Where the United States was once the international leader in granting college degrees, we've now fallen to 10th. (1)

Adelman and Carey went on to note that state revenues were drying up and that the chances of new money arising in the near future were slim to none in the depths of the recession. In such an economic environment, they argued states had little choice but to "improve the way they fund and govern higher education. To give all students the best possible postsecondary education, states must create smart, effective higher education accountability systems" (1).

An obvious question arises here: What might smart and effective accountability systems look like? For Adelman and Carey, "The laboratories of democracy" (a version of American ingenuity perhaps), as they put it, "have produced a wide range of methods" for assessing key areas of accountability: student learning, institutional practices, and economic and community development (2). A key facet of accountability, as they argued, includes focusing on efficiency and financial stewardship, which is to be expected in good times and bad; after all, public universities should be held accountable to their publics and should not waste state tax revenue. More times than not, though, efficiency and financial stewardship in the shadows of the Great Recession were translated into calls to reduce full-time faculty and increase faculty workload. In terms of the former, the casualization of the academic workforce had already begun a decade or so earlier (Johnson and McCarthy 2000), but arguably it became even more entrenched in the thinking of administrators and policy makers following the economic crisis of the early twenty-first century (Gilbert 2013). The second common strategy—attacking faculty workload—often was tied to an assumption that faculty enjoyed a cushy life and presumably had plenty of free time to teach more courses. Both strategies of course aimed to lower the production costs of the most basic higher education commodity—the university course.

With students and parents struggling to make ends meet, and states struggling to pay their bills, critics of faculty workload along with advocates of faculty performance outcomes found growing support. One of the loudest critics was Richard Vedder, an economist at Ohio University and adjunct scholar at the American Enterprise Institute. Vedder noted time and time again the amount of wasted investment in U.S. higher education, to a great extent linking it to the lack of productivity of faculty, especially among those working in the social sciences and humanities (Vedder 2011).[6] As pressure increased, numerous universities and state systems took heed. Texas A&M University assumed center stage with its highly criticized "bottom-line" ratings, scoring faculty on the basis of revenue generated (e.g., course enrollments and research dollars) minus costs (essentially their salaries). The outcome was mostly good, at least for the majority of faculty: "Faculty members at Texas A&M University are, by and large, generating more money than they are costing the university, although some of the most prestigious professors would appear to be operating in the red" (Mangan 2010). Public universities in Texas were particularly vulnerable, with the University of Texas adopting a plan to publish performance data about faculty, including "publications, teaching evaluations, and external support" (Mangan 2011). Other states also pushed for greater accountability of faculty work, seeking to increase faculty workload. Furthermore, a Chronicle-Moody's survey of nearly five hundred college and university chief financial officers indicated that 38 percent supported raising teaching loads as the greatest source of cost savings. Also worth noting, three of the next four top strategies for addressing financial problems targeted faculty labor, arguing for the elimination of tenure, hiring more adjuncts, and adopting a mandatory retirement age (Bauerlein 2011).

Under intense scrutiny, it seemed reasonable that calls for increased online education, through such innovations as the MOOC, became more palatable, perhaps even to those professors who months or years earlier might have scoffed at such an idea. This is not to suggest that the rise of the MOOC was accompanied by faculty joining arms with efficiency-minded administrators, online education innovators, and instructional technology staff for a chorus of "Kumbaya." Instead, my point is that difficult financial conditions for higher education contributed to a strong push for greater accountability, including calls for increased faculty productivity, and that these trends arose during a time in which there was growing acceptance of online education more generally. Under such conditions, increasing an institution's engagement in online education arose as a possible solution, as was indicated by results from KPMG's third annual Higher Education Outlook survey, wherein 43 percent of senior administrative officers said their college or university planned to expand online courses as an "antidote" to declines in funding (Chronicle Staff 2014). Thus, multiple forces combined to form a perfect storm, resulting in more fertile soil for planting and growing the seeds of a potentially cost-saving and transformative educational innovation—the MOOC.

Dawn of the MOOC

In 2008 George Siemens and Stephen Downes, both working out of Canada, offered an open online course at the University of Manitoba on the topic of connectivist learning theory called "Connectivism and Connectivist Knowledge," also known as CCK08.[7] Although a group of about two dozen students took the course for credit through the university's extension program, roughly 2,300 additional noncredit learners participated in the course as well. CCK08 was a huge success by nearly every measure imaginable, serving as a signpost in the changing landscape of online education. The *Chronicle of Higher Education* noted the significance of the course in August 2010, pointing out that this new type of course "even spawned a new name: Massive Open Online Course, or MOOC" (Parry 2010).[8] The course Siemens and Downes designed, and the MOOC movement to which they both contributed, was based in part on a theory of connectivist learning advanced to a great extent by Siemens. Connectivist learning theory attempts to capture the ways in which learners develop and nurture social connections through various networks, including Internet-based networks, as a means to extend their knowledge and understanding in today's world (Siemens 2004). This theory and its relevance to the MOOC movement, specifically in terms of connectivist MOOCs, or cMOOCs, are discussed in much detail in chapter 3. Suffice to say for now that Siemens and his contribution to connectivist learning theory had a significant impact on the rise and expansion of the MOOC movement. His conviction in Web-based teaching and learning as a vehicle for deep and meaningful engagement among networks of collaborative teachers and learners (or producers and users) helped to change the world of online education.

The OER movement helped to promote widespread sharing of information and knowledge, including the development of various course platforms such as Moodle, Google's Open Course Builder, and OpenMOOC, among others. Such trends in OER were combined with a variety of technological shifts, including advances associated with Web 2.0, and paved the way for university efforts to make course materials available online, resulting in the rise of OCW, led initially by MIT OpenCourseWare. Thus, it was the coming together of new technologies and emergent notions of shared knowledge (including software sharing) that undergirded the rise of MOOCs and furthered the innovative thinking of online education advocates such as Downes and Siemens. Additionally, globalization and the advance of transnational higher education markets helped to make online innovations such as MOOCs that much more appealing, given their potential to reach countless learners, who in the context of a global economic crisis and a strong push toward marketization were increasingly defined as potential consumers. Although they were hardly advocates of a consumerist model of online education, Downes and Siemens clearly understood the growing impact of globalized educational forms.

Although Siemens was a key figure in the development of MOOCs, others also played major roles, including the aforementioned Stephen Downes and John Seely Brown but also Cathy Davidson and David Wiley, among others. Davidson discussed aspects of "MOOC Madness" in a 2013 essay published with HASTAC (Humanities, Arts, Science, and Technology Alliance and Collaboratory) while also raising critical concerns about potential institutional inequities, some of which are central to the narrative unfolding in this book. As she put it: "Will professors at underfunded state universities and small liberal arts colleges all be replaced by a few dozen elite profs blabbing away from some laptop? Are MOOCs a 'game changer' for higher education that, in fact, spells 'game over': Will MOOCs destroy the financial structure of the professorate and the very fiber of learning—all that is interactive, immediate, human, loving, and great about learning?" Davidson, who developed and taught her own MOOC—"The History and Future of Higher Education" (2014a)—tends to bring a critical eye to her analysis of the MOOC movement, while also acknowledging the very serious problems confronting today's higher education systems, including what she sees as the need for a paradigm shift and higher education's lack of urgency in adopting a more open and collaborative model of teaching and learning—akin to some extent to the Wikipedia model stressing the "features of open-contributive knowledge-sharing" (2014b, 5).

Wiley maintains a blog addressing topics related to online education and MOOCs as part of what he calls "iterating toward openness." In one blog titled "What's the Difference Between OCWs and MOOCs? Managing Expectations," Wiley (2013) argued that what largely separates the two is linked to "market positioning and expectation management." On the one hand, he saw OCW mostly as teacher oriented, which is different from the positioning of MOOCs. Wiley elaborated on this position:

> MIT OCW has always positioned itself as primarily teacher-facing. The collections of materials are intended to support faculty at other institutions in teaching similar classes or engaging in professional development. When independent learners manage to benefit from MIT OCW, this is a happy coincidence—a secondary benefit of the primary mission of supporting faculty around the world. Since MIT OCW is teacher-facing, of course there is no faculty member there to support students. Only the very bright and extremely self-motivated can benefit, but that's ok since serving students isn't their actual mission.

On the other hand, as Wiley clarified, MOOCs are more oriented toward serving the needs of students, or learners more broadly conceived. MOOC providers, namely the commercial ones, "positioned themselves as primarily student-facing." Their online materials were mainly about supporting student learning, and often times their "Terms of Service explicitly prohibit faculty around the world from using their materials in the courses they teach (there will be no secondary benefits)." Because the goal is to advance student learning, the reality of limited instructional support becomes more problematic than in the OCW world, where teachers and more advanced learners tend to negotiate the materials on their own. He went on to add, "The idea that only the very bright and extremely self-motivated can benefit from . . . MOOCs, which is what appears to be happening, is problematic since serving learners is their stated mission."

I find Wiley's commentary helpful in differentiating basic yet confusing differences between OCW and MOOCs. However, the diversity of MOOCs is not entirely accounted for in Wiley's critique, given that increasingly MOOCs have found ways to expand forms of instructional support. I say more about this in chapter 3, when I highlight MOOC-related teaching and learning issues and discuss in detail cMOOCs and xMOOCs.

Wiley (2013) raised an important issue when he pointed out that the eventual backlash arising to challenge MOOCs was in part the result of the different ways in which the two movements managed expectations. He posed this basic question: Why did we eventually see an anti-MOOC backlash but not an anti-OCW backlash? He then answered his own question: "Perhaps because even though to the public mind they're doing essentially the same things—publishing large collections of curated, high quality, freely available course content—OCW managed the public's expectations better." In terms of the latter point, OCW advocates did not make the same kind of grandiose claims that some of the biggest MOOC advocates made—especially the more entrepreneurial ones. To this I add that OCW never had the revenue-generating potential that MOOCs offered, in that the OCW movement was mostly framed in the spirit of the knowledge commons, as part of the democratization of knowledge and information. Although MOOCs too had roots in the ideals of the knowledge commons, they also caught the fancy of venture capitalists, entrepreneurs, and revenue-minded educationalists who saw a potential revenue model in the form of online massification of course credit and credentialing.

At the heart of both OCW and MOOCs, then, is the effort to make course materials more widely available either for teachers or for learners. Both may include reading lists, assignments, videos, recorded lectures, lecture notes, quizzes, exams, and so forth. But MOOCs may also pose the possibility of joining study groups, giving and receiving feedback in conjunction with other online learners, or participating in a discussion of sorts, perhaps in the form of a chat room, discussion board, or through the use of social media. Ideally, MOOCs seek to build on the principles of connectivism and connectivist knowledge (through forms of social learning), as Siemen stressed in his concept of the cMOOC. However, the vast majority of MOOCs are unlikely to have this social learning quality; they tend to convey ideas and information from instructor to student in more traditional one-directional formats, such as through postings on a course website. This latter type of MOOC is often described as an xMOOC, in that it lacks many of the important connectivist learning features of cMOOCs and is far more easily implemented on a massive scale.

A strength of the xMOOC and the primary role it has come to play in the higher education arena is that it fosters access to courses and course materials for thousands of learners at a time. Its capacity to extend higher education to broad and expansive populations, including students already enrolled in university programs, is the central reason why xMOOCs have drawn so much attention from both higher education policy makers and entrepreneurs, including venture capitalists.

Several entrepreneurial-mined MOOC advocates come to mind, including Stanford University research professor Sebastian Thrun, who, collaborating with Peter Norvig, director of research at Google, initially attracted 160,000 online learners to his artificial intelligence (AI) course (Selingo 2014; Young 2013). The popularity of the Thrun-Norvig AI course "exploded online, drawing students from around the world" (DeSantis 2012). The initial MOOC experience helped Thrun imagine a new world of higher education in which the interactive tools of Web 2.0 could be harnessed to create a feeling of face-to-face tutoring among online learners. Inspired by the success of his AI MOOC, in early 2011 Thrun founded Udacity, a start-up company that he envisioned offering low-cost online courses, taking full advantage of Internet-based technologies. Thrun argued that universities were light-years behind in how they teach, still stressing the lecture format. He pointed to countless technological innovations such as "the invention of celluloid, of digital media" and criticized contemporary professors who he said "miraculously . . . teach exactly the same way they taught a thousand years ago" (DeSantis 2012). Thrun eventually gave up teaching at Stanford (he did not give up his research position), focusing more of his energy on developing and promoting courses for Udacity, such as a seven-week course on building a search engine.

Stanford figured quite prominently in the world of the MOOC and the related expansion of online learning. In addition to Thrun, Daphne Koller and Andrew Ng, faculty in Stanford's Computer Science Department, founded Coursera on the basis of their success offering online courses, most notably Ng's machine learning course. Koller and Ng captured the imagination of venture capitalists and journalists alike, with *Time* magazine including both among "The 100 Most Influential People in the World" for 2013. The one thing all three shared, in addition to their brilliance in their chosen fields, was brashness in proclaiming the revolutionary potential of MOOCs. At one point in 2012 Thrun predicted that in fifty years there would likely be only ten higher education institutions left standing, with Udacity having a good chance of being one of them (Leckart 2012). Only time will tell, but Thrun was much less sanguine roughly a year later, following a debacle at San Jose State University, when Udacity's efforts to offer remedial math courses mostly failed (Schuman 2013). Writing for a blog called *Hack Education*, Audrey Watters (2013a) went so far as to prognosticate Thrun's "Last 10 Standing":

1. Oxford
2. Cambridge
3. Harvard
4. MIT
5. Stanford
6. Princeton
7. The University of Google (acquires Udacity, 2014)
8. The University of Pearson (acquires Coursera, 2016)
9. The University of Walmart (acquires University of Phoenix, 2017)
10. Brigham Young University

Perhaps the sarcasm was fair, given the wild claims of the entrepreneurial-minded MOOC advocates. Even Siemens expressed dismay at the brashness of Thrun in particular, noting in 2013, "No one will do more damage to MOOCs as a concept than Thrun now that he realizes how unfounded his statements actually were" (Kolowich 2014c). These comments came after Thrun backtracked in his thinking about MOOCs "democratizing" higher education and increasingly turned to applying MOOCs to the realm of corporate training.

In some sense, it's hard to fault Thrun and others for what later seemed like untempered optimism, a bit overly ambitious and perhaps somewhat naive. After all, MOOC Madness was intoxicating. The excessive hype associated with MOOCs is what Wiley (2013) referred to when he astutely pointed out that where OCW advocates had managed expectations, MOOC supporters had gone over the edge. This is not to suggest that MOOCs do not have promise, but clearly a more tempered analysis is needed. Thus, a central goal of this book is to move beyond the rhetoric of MOOCs revolutionizing higher education and instead critically analyze their educational possibilities.

Concluding Thoughts

Central to explaining the emergence of MOOCs are complex and dynamic cultural, economic, and technological changes taking place mostly in the late 1990s and early 2000s, including enhancements to the World Wide Web resulting in the potential for greater social learning and connectivity. Concurrently, emerging ideals relating to a more democratic take on the role of information and knowledge relative to serving the broader social good emerged and were applied to the Internet in the form of the knowledge commons. Thus, the emergence of Web 2.0 technologies in combination with the ideological shift in how knowledge was viewed converged to help give rise to the OER movement and soon thereafter OCW initiatives. The emergence of OCW and mindsets linked to the knowledge commons helped establish supportive conditions for the emergence of the MOOC, as part of the advance of a more democratic vision of the university course. Stressful financial conditions linked to the Great Recession along with greater openness to online education also furthered conditions conducive to educational innovations such as the MOOC.

Although early MOOC thinkers envisioned a more advanced and connectivist form of adult and continuing education, other entrepreneurial types saw the potential for massification, cost savings, and revenue flows. And so early on the MOOC movement underwent rapid changes, including expansion in size and impact. With its phenomenal growth arose growing criticism, especially on the part of faculty. In part, a certain degree of skepticism was warranted, given some of the wild claims by early educational entrepreneurs caught up in what they saw as the revolutionary potential of MOOCs. A positive result though was that a level of sanity slowly entered into the discourse, as MOOC Madness gave way to more reasonable considerations and expectations. At least this is how it all seemed by 2014, when I took on this present assignment. In the world of high-tech revolutions, though, no one knows what the next few years will bring. And so in concluding this opening chapter I feel obligated to remind readers that the world of the MOOC is a moving target and this book offers a portrait during one particular sliver of time, namely from 2008 through 2014.

In chapter 2—"The Organizational System of the World of the MOOC"—I offer an extensive analysis of the key organizational players arising to propel the MOOC movement, including the basic organizational structure undergirding the phenomenon. A key aspect of this chapter centers on the coming together of both public good and more privatized enterprises in helping to strengthen the movement. In chapter 3—"Connectivism, Social Learning, and the cMOOC/xMOOC Distinction"—I focus on key teaching and learning issues related to the emergence and expansion of MOOCs, including the importance of connectivist principles arising from the earliest MOOCs. I point to some of the shortcomings associated with xMOOCs, while also noting the possibilities for success. Chapter 4—"Blowback and Resistance to the MOOC Movement"—centers on a more critical analysis of MOOCs, including a discussion of five basic problems: (1) the problem of epistemology, (2) the problem of pedagogy, (3) the problem of hegemony, (4) the problem of diversity, and (5) the problem of faculty labor. I argue that these five problems associated with MOOCs undermine the movement's growth and dampen much of the initial enthusiasm for MOOCs as a transformative force. Finally, I conclude in chapter 5—"The Future of MOOCs and Higher Learning"—with a more realistic discussion of the role of MOOCs in higher education's future, while also raising important concerns about higher learning in an age of high technology. I also advance the idea of a hybrid MOOC in the form of the xsMOOC. I conclude chapter 5 by highlighting practical concerns and implications of MOOCs for higher education broadly speaking, for faculty members, and for national and state-level organizations involved in the higher education arena.

2

The Organizational System
of the World of the MOOC

A complex array of social actors and organizations came to form an organizational system undergirding the emergence and advance of the MOOC movement. A key facet of the system was the convergence of both private and public good interests that at times are complementary while at other times contradictory. This mix of public good and private interests—the latter captured most significantly by the large amount of funds poured into MOOC start-ups by venture capital (VC) firms—represents a unique set of circumstances, including partnerships between for-profit enterprises, such as Coursera, with nonprofit universities (Selingo 2014; Young 2013). Although not entirely unusual, this mix of for-profit and nonprofit entities presents added organizational and systemic complexities, including potential tensions between public good and for-profit motives. That a complex organizational system came to play a crucial role in the MOOC movement underscores the dynamism and complexity of change within the contemporary higher education arena. Furthermore, understanding the nature of the actors and organizations constituting such a system is critical to analyzing the overall significance and potential of MOOCs as an educational reform movement.

The convergence of both public good and private interests in support of the MOOC movement is a key consideration of this chapter. On the one hand, OER/OCW advocates voiced a strong commitment to the public good potential of MOOCs to further democratize higher education, a position consistent with the ideals of the knowledge commons. As state and federal support for colleges and universities wavered, MOOCs held the potential to help higher education institutions maintain their social contract with a demanding public by making university courses more accessible. On the other hand, venture capitalists and entrepreneurs recognized the growing demand for higher education and the reality that online education was increasingly seen as part of the solution to limited brick-and-mortar access. An example here was the strong support of venture capitalists in the founding of for-profit enterprises such as Coursera and Udacity (Walsh 2011). Those supporting a private-enterprise model also employed the discourse of "democratizing higher education," but at the same time they clearly saw the revenue potential of MOOCs given the ability to replicate courses on a massive scale while minimizing course production costs. Institutional cost savings were largely tied to the potential of reducing salaries paid to course designers and instructors (typically faculty members). Simply put, paying one faculty member to create and teach a course for ten thousand students seemed much cheaper than the prevailing course-production model. Although the two groups employed a similar discourse at times—that of democratizing higher education—there were in fact significant differences between those advocating MOOCs as a public good versus those envisioning their revenue-generating potential. Thus, there were times when public good concerns and private interests came together to support further development of MOOCs, and there were times when they were at odds. Adding to the complexity of the emergent organizational system was the growing influence of globalization and the reality of higher education as a transnational endeavor increasingly constituted as a global market.

The organizational system I describe in this chapter includes six basic entities: MOOC users, course producers, course providers, legitimizers, funders, and networks/associations. I stress the interactivity of this system and the fact that some entities play multiple roles. Take for example the Gates Foundation, which both serves as a funder for the MOOC movement and acts to legitimize MOOCs as an educational innovation. This sort of complication must be kept in mind, as the system I describe is conceptual in nature and cannot possibly capture the full complexity of the MOOC movement and its underlying structure.

Before moving on to discuss the organizational system and the six types of entities undergirding the MOOC movement, it is helpful to highlight critical organizational developments that paved the way for MOOCs, including the important role for-profits played as front runners in the online education arena. The early role of several elite nonprofit universities and their experimentation with online education also was critical to framing the eventual organizational context giving rising to MOOCs.

Early Organizational Developments

The first decade of the twenty-first century saw online education emerge as a key strategy for meeting consumer needs as the demand for higher education continued to grow. Indeed, for many in the for-profit higher education industry, where online education was widely embraced as legitimate teaching and learning strategy, it was a bull market. For-profit institutions such as DeVry, Kaplan, Strayer, and the University of Phoenix (the Apollo Group) performed exceedingly well financially in an environment in which online learners seemed endless in number. However, the bull market was challenged in 2010 when elected officials led by Iowa senator Tom Harkin launched a two-year investigation of the for-profit industry by the U.S. Senate Committee on Health, Education, Labor, and Pensions (HELP). The eventual 2012 HELP report criticized the for-profit industry on the basis that a good deal of the profit taking came at the expense of the nation's taxpayers, given that many for-profits depended on the federal student financial aid program. This shift in the regulatory landscape contributed to a decline in profits within the sector. Perhaps lost among the criticism of the for-profits was the reality that nonprofit colleges and universities increasingly considered more aggressive strategies for reaching scores of online learners.

The weakened position of the for-profits in the aftermath of increased scrutiny from Congress highlights the fact that higher education is not a pure market but is heavily subsidized by the federal government, particularly in terms of the national student financial aid program. Further, criticism by the U.S. Senate of the for-profit sector highlighted how federal tax dollars were being utilized to heavily support the industry, with many for-profits earning as much as 90 percent of their total revenue through the federal student loan program. Data from the U.S. Department of Education for the 2010–11 academic year showed that 372 for-profits earned 85 to 90 percent of their revenue from federal student aid, placing them in the danger zone with regard to the 90/10 rule, while another 15 failed to meet the rule (Kingkade 2012); the 90/10 rule puts a 90 percent limit on how much an institution participating in the federal financial aid program can collect from government sources. In all, data revealed that for-profits collected $32 billion from the federal government in the 2010–11 year.

Although much of their revenue was generated by face-to-face courses, for-profits were aggressive in developing online programs as well. For example, fall

2012 data from the National Center for Education Statistics (NCES) pointed out that four-year for-profits led the way in enrolling students exclusively in distance education courses with over 900,000, accounting for roughly 61 percent of their overall enrollment. In contrast, about 7 percent of all students at four-year public universities and 12 percent at four-year privates were exclusively distance education students.[1] The report, sponsored by the U.S. Department of Education (2014), noted the importance of this data offering "a useful baseline for tracking future trends, particularly as certain states and institutions focus on MOOCs and other distance education initiatives" (1). Given the growing influence of the MOOC movement on the nonprofit sector specifically, it seems reasonable to expect that the engagement of students in distance education programs is likely to increase significantly in the coming years. This is likely to lead to increased competition for students among institutions offering online courses and programs in both the for-profit and nonprofit sectors.

My point in discussing the for-profit sector is to highlight two critical roles it played in laying the organizational foundation for further innovations in online education, including the development of MOOCs. First, for-profits highlight key facets of the public-private tension prevalent also in the MOOC movement. As for-profit entities, these institutions exist primarily to make money. But they also serve a public good function in expanding college access for certain segments of the higher education consumer population, and of course they do so by reaping the benefits of public tax dollars through the national student financial aid program. Second, for-profits were quick to see the potential of online education, demonstrating in practice the viability of distance education courses and programs conducted primarily online. Their experience in this arena contributed in significant ways to the eventual attraction to online education by nonprofit colleges and universities. Enthusiasm over the possibilities of online education also increased with enhancements associated with Web 2.0, as the technological changes presented more sophisticated options in the development of online course materials.

Yale was one of the first nonprofit universities to explore online education in a big way, entering into a joint venture with Oxford, Princeton, and Stanford in 2001 to create AllLearn, a nonprofit that sought to further develop online education with the idea of developing possible revenue models. When the venture failed only a few years later, in 2007, Yale began focusing on its own online offerings, seeking to develop a small group of free user-friendly courses based largely on recorded lectures from highly regarded professors. Columbia, around 2000, also created its own online education portal in the form of Fathom, a for-profit consortium partnering with the London School of Economics and Political Science, the British Library, and the New York Public Library, among others. But Fathom closed after only three years when it failed to turn a profit. Although both AllLearn and Fathom failed to successfully develop revenue-producing models of online education, they nonetheless played an important role in helping educators, innovators, and entrepreneurs better understand the challenges and limitations of online education.

One critical point to take from the experiments of AllLearn and Fathom is that online courses offered by elite universities are not necessarily a big enough draw to charge fees if not linked to credentialing, as in offering a certificate or degree program (this is not intended as a commentary on MOOCs, as they tend to be free and elite universities have attracted thousands of users to them). Elite universities such as Columbia and Yale were reluctant to connect their online offerings to credential or degree programs for fear of damaging their brands. Some exceptions, though, included top research universities such as Pennsylvania State University and Michigan State University, which created a wide range of online degree-earning programs and even marketed them globally in the case of Penn State World Campus.

Generally speaking, though, the foray of elite universities into the online education arena was met mostly with failure, leading several leading universities to consider a new vision—offering courses or course materials for free, perhaps as part of their public service mission as nonprofit organizations. Again, MIT OpenCourseWare was the forerunner for this version of online education, but others, including Carnegie Mellon University in Pittsburgh, offered contributions to the growth of this emerging model and eventual movement. CMU, taking advantage of its expertise in cognitive and computer sciences, developed a small group of high-quality, high-tech open courses through its Open Learning Initiative (OLI). This model of open online education was much different from that of MIT OCW, the latter simply making a wide range of course materials including syllabi available online (the goal was to make every course syllabus available). CMU instead sought to spend much more money—roughly $500,000 to $1 million per course—developing quite sophisticated learning experiences, including "cognitive tutors, virtual laboratories, group experiments and simulations" (Atkins, Brown, and Hammond 2007, 12). There were, however, limitations to the CMU model: The basic view of knowledge tended to be foundationalist in nature, in that courses stressed static knowledge. Forms of teaching and learning linked to more collaborative and constructivist models of education could not be so easily managed by computer software, although AI devotees often disagree with this assertion. The promise of CMU's AI-influenced MOOCs were the likely reason that in June 2014, Google, through its Focused Research Award program, granted the university $300,000 a year for two years with the possibility of a third to focus on further developing computer-based automatic approaches to providing feedback on student work. A CMU news release described the goal of the project "to develop platforms intelligent enough to mimic the traditional classroom experience" (Wolfman-Arent 2014). Obviously, efforts were being made to develop more complex feedback mechanisms in light of the shortcomings of computer-scored multiple choice quizzes and exams.

With more universities offering open online courses, ranging from MIT's course materials to Yale's recorded lectures and CMU's cognitively advanced offerings, the stage was set for other players to enter the arena by providing an array of services to online learners. Credentialing was one service eventually developed, with various entities emerging to offer badges, certificates, and even degrees in some cases. If elites such as MIT, Yale, and CMU were not willing to award online course completers with certificates or degrees, then other organizations were more than happy to do so—for a slight fee of course, at least in most cases. With the need to affirm a level of educational attainment by online learners claiming to have completed an open course, it was necessary to develop systems for verifying learning outcomes. Course work completed by an online learner, and the related learning outcomes, needed to be comparable in some manner or form with an actual face-to-face university course. Otherwise, how could one earn legitimate course credit or a meaningful badge or certificate? With such concerns arising, private companies such as Pearson VUE testing emerged to offer a variety of services for confirming student learning outcomes. Additionally, nonprofit organizations such as the American Council on Education came to the forefront in approving online courses as legitimate university-level learning experiences. Major supporters of online education, such as the Gates and Hewlett foundations, added to what increasingly took on the appearance of a dynamic social movement, complete with an array of organizations and key social actors undergirding it. What emerged near the end of the first decade of the twenty-first century was a complex organizational system focused in large part on transforming higher education. Surely, higher education would never be the same.

A Complex Organizational System

The structure that emerged to undergird first the OCW movement and then later MOOCs may be considered in terms of several functional and intersecting roles, creating what amounts to a complex organizational system.[2] These functional roles include the following six types of entities: MOOC users, course producers, course providers, legitimizers, funders, and networks/associations. In what follows, I first offer a structural analysis of the OCW/MOOC movements, outlining and discussing the form of the organizational system that served to support these movements. I then move on to offer a more critical analysis of competing tensions within the system, namely the tension between public good and private capital initiatives. The organizational system that I describe is best understood as arising within the context of high demand for higher education, reduced or stagnant governmental funding, advances in Web technologies, and a powerful mix of public good and private enterprise interests.

MOOC Users

I begin with the most basic of all key actors in the rise of any demand-driven movement—the actual users, or to borrow from business parlance, the consumers. Higher education in the first decade of the twenty-first century was a business in great demand, especially at a global level. Numerous policy analysts and economists, including Gary Becker (2013) of the University of Chicago, described a "worldwide boom" in higher education. From Brazil, to China, to India, to the United States, higher education institutions had a difficult time meeting the demands of prospective students in the first decade and a half of the twenty-first century. Increased enrollment by female students and nontraditional learners added significantly to the pool of prospective students. Furthermore, advances in Web technologies made geographic barriers in some sense nonexistent; the growing reach of online education contributed to its expanding role globally.

What is known about the users of online courses? Or more to the point, what is known about those who take a MOOC? First of all, the dropout rate is incredibly high for MOOCs, and just as incredibly misleading. Yes, the vast majority who enroll in a MOOC—as high as 97 percent in some cases—do not complete the course. But this may not be a reflection of the quality of the learning experience as much as it is the ease of participation, which for some may be nothing more than curiosity-seeking behavior. As one writer noted, "People who register for MOOCs are said to include precocious high school students . . . [and] college students looking for more ways to study a subject they are learning in a traditional classroom" (Rivard 2013a). Research out of MIT on some of the first MOOCs also suggested that how we think about MOOC enrollment and retention cannot be based on traditional measures of course success, such as whether or not someone actually completes a course. Instead, course assessment data must analyze differential tracts reflecting diverse user goals (De-Boer, Ho, Stump, and Breslow 2014). This is not unlike formulas for assessing community college student retention, given the diverse goals such students often have when enrolling in courses. For example, it makes no sense to compare the degree completion rates of community college students enrolled for professional development purposes with other students seeking an associate of arts degree with the goal of transferring to a four-year college or university; the former group may include students who enroll in one course and never show up again, yet fully achieve their professional development objectives. The same type of considerations must be applied to MOOC users, whose educational interests and learning objectives may be even more diverse than those of students typically attending community colleges.

Studies suggest that a distinction needs to be made between course enrollees and active students. A report from the University of London International Programmes defined active students "as unique users who viewed or downloaded a lecture, attempted a quiz, registered after the MOOC start date and/or posted on the MOOC forums" (Grainger 2013, 27). Empirical studies in the United States confirm this perspective, generally noting that MOOC users include a range of participants who may have marginal interest in actually completing the course, including other teachers looking to enhance their instructional skills and repertoires. The London report also noted that about 50 percent of students who enroll in advance for a MOOC don't even bother showing up. As the report highlighted, "Most MOOCs shed roughly 50% of their registered students by the time the course starts" (27).

Basic geographic data about MOOC users also exists. Based on data from HarvardX, the university's division for online education, there were 572,899 registrants in 18 HarvardX courses representing 206 countries, with the largest percentage of users being from the United States (42%) and then India (9.5%), followed by Canada (less than 4%) (Nesterko et al. 2014). Language appears to be an important factor, with six of the top ten countries in terms of enrollment representing ones in which more than 50 percent of the population speaks English.

A couple of studies reported that MOOC users are mostly males, but these studies were conducted in computer science–based MOOCs, and computer science is a field highly dominated by men. For example, MIT researchers examined data from the famously popular course "Circuits and Electronics," edX's first MOOC, and found that 88 percent of the users were male. The study also noted that 67 percent spoke English, with the next largest language group being Spanish at 16 percent. Of the over 1,100 who responded to a survey, 55 percent had a bachelor's, master's, or professional degree, while 27 percent had a high school degree (Breslow et al. 2013).

A study conducted at the University of Pennsylvania confirmed high educational attainment levels among MOOC users, noting that 83 percent of course enrollees had either a two- or four-year degree (Christensen et al. 2013).[3] This study surveyed 34,779 students worldwide from 24 courses offered through Penn's Open Learning Initiative operated in partnership with Coursera; at the time of the study, enrollment in Penn's OLI courses accounted for more than 20 percent of Coursera's total enrollment across its partner institutions. The study also reported that most of Penn's MOOC students were male (56.9%) and either employed full-time or self-employed (62.4%). The two main reasons given for enrolling in a MOOC were professional development and curiosity. The relevance of curiosity as a source of motivation may help to explain why such a low percentage of MOOC users actually complete a course, given that one's curiosity may be satisfied simply through exploring facets of a MOOC asynchronously. Another study focusing on the nature of student engagement among more than 1 million users in Penn's OLI courses supports the preceding assertion, arguing that "The 'open' nature of MOOCs assumes that benefits may result even from sporadic participation, as those who 'lurk' may access substantial amounts of course content and realize meaningful learning opportunities" (Perna et al. 2013, 2). From such a perspective, data revealing low completion rates should be interpreted cautiously. Audrey Watters said it nicely: "People fail to complete these courses for lots of reasons, but it's important to highlight one in particular: What makes these courses so easy to sign up for makes them just as easy to drop. MOOCs have no barriers to entry—no fees, no prerequisites, no textbooks. If you bail out, there's no record on your transcript or financial aid to pay back. You come, you go" (2012, 6).

A final point of note concerning the Penn findings is the fact that the online users MOOCs are primarily designed to help were greatly underrepresented among actual course takers (Christensen et al. 2013). Although this finding was likely influenced to an extent by the professional development focus of many of the OLI courses (Perna et al. 2013), other studies have reported similar findings (Breslow et al. 2013). This point is particularly relevant given that many of the early MOOC entrepreneurs spoke of democratizing higher education, presumably by reaching out to non–degree holders.

Course Producers

At the most basic level college and university professors and Internet-based educational innovators have been the driving force in the development of open online course content and course-related materials. The term "open" is critical to my point here. I recognize that for-profits and a host of highly accessible public universities and more entrepreneurial private institutions aggressively pursued the development of online courses long before professors at elite universities such as Yale and MIT were involved in open courseware initiatives. Indeed, the rise of the for-profit sector was in many ways built on the "disruptive innovations" associated with online education (Tierney and Hentschke 2007). Such innovations, however, were not open courses in the sense of being free or feeless; they were ventures designed to capitalize on the Internet and the perceived financial advantages of scalable courses. The course producers highlighted in this section are of a different ilk, working in a different environment. They are faculty and educational innovators involved in the development of open courses, emerging largely as part of the OER and OCW movements. These mostly were educators operating on the conviction that knowledge and information should be made readily available *en masse*; recognizing the power of the Internet, they chose to share their course resources openly.

Many of the course producers offer a complete collection of course materials, including digitally recorded lectures, lecture notes, PowerPoint slides, reading lists, quizzes, exams, and so forth. The more technologically advanced open courses may also include sophisticated learning options such as simulations, game-like environments, and perhaps even group-oriented assignments, typically with quite minimal instructional support. Some MOOCs encourage course users to develop their own learning communities, including providing feedback to one another regarding various assignments (peer assessment). In many cases, certain materials are only available during the period in which the course is actually taught (most MOOCs are synchronous), although materials such as syllabi often may be accessed for extended periods of time.

Certain course content producers, such as those contributing digitally recorded lectures, have achieved much notoriety. A good example here is Michael Sandel, a professor of political philosophy at Harvard, whose entertaining lectures on justice have made him somewhat of a rock star in Asia. A June 2011 *New York Times* op-ed by Thomas Friedman captured his stardom:

> You probably missed the recent special issue of *China Newsweek*, so let me bring you up to date. Who do you think was on the cover—named the "most influential foreign figure" of the year in China? Barack Obama? No. Bill Gates? No. Warren Buffett? No. O.K., I'll give you a hint: He's a rock star in Asia, and people in China, Japan and South Korea scalp tickets to hear him. Give up?

Other MOOC course producers such as Stanford's Andrew Ng, Daphne Koller, Sebastian Thrun, and Peter Norvig have also received a good deal of attention, mostly in the form of media coverage of the MOOC movement that they helped to propel. Some of these faculty members also went on to found key MOOC providers such as Coursera and Udacity.

The reality, though, is that most MOOC producers do not achieve the stardom of Koller or Thrun; they simply are committed to a vision of the world congruent with the knowledge commons. They believe that all interested learners should have access to sets of course materials useful for their self-defined learning goals.

A final point to make here is that MOOCs are not simply course materials offered for free online—that is essentially OCW. MOOCs go beyond OCW and are likely to have synchronous qualities while incorporating forms of instruction, whether offered by real teachers or through social learning mechanisms, wherein online learners offer tutorials and other forms of support to one another. MOOCs may seek out volunteer instructors, tutors, and other support staff—typically people who already have knowledge of the subject under study. An example here is Coursera's use of Community Teaching Assistants in some of its MOOCs; Community TAs are students who have previously done well in a course and then are asked to voluntarily assist others in a next iteration of the course. This type of MOOC volunteer model is revealed in an ad by the MOOC provider Open Doors Group (ODG), posted at their website in June 2013:

Open Doors Group is seeking volunteer staff for its upcoming Massive Open Online Courses (MOOCs). Benefits to volunteers include MOOC experience, learning the popular Canvas Learning Management System (LMS), networking with educators and others, possible academic paper, references, and more. We are testing an interesting MOOC freemium business model: provide the courses at no charge and sell the very affordable textbooks. The classes are in the autumn and work is already in progress. About 20–30 hours are needed from each volunteer. Instructional designers and instructors are needed now; editors and testers in August.[4]

In addition to capturing the volunteer or public service facet of producing MOOCs, the ODG posting also offers a sense of the kind of revenue-generating experimentation linked to MOOCs; in this case, ODG hoped to raise money through sales of textbooks.

Although MOOCs are likely to offer forms of instructional support, the reality is that mechanisms for support built into courses by MOOC producers are usually rather minimal. This is in part tied to the basic idea that MOOCs usually aim to be massive and operate on an economy-of-scale model; hence, providing intensive instructional assistance is likely to be too time consuming and require a financial payment for the course instructor. In turn, having to pay an instructor (or instructors) is likely to necessitate fees for course participants. Once a fee is charged, the MOOC simply becomes an online course, and the basic ideals of the knowledge commons are undermined. Given these production issues, minimizing instructional costs is critical to MOOCs and the intent of most MOOC providers.

MOOC Providers

A third category of social actor, in this case an organizational entity, is what I call MOOC providers (sometimes also described as "platforms"), not to be confused with MOOC producers. Producers are mostly individual faculty members who design and teach MOOCs, whereas providers are organizations that support the development of MOOCs, build a collection or list of MOOC offerings, and then make them available to online users or learners. MOOC providers may also offer additional services, including credentialing in some cases, with such services often involving a fee. Providers serve as consolidators for the overall MOOC movement, bringing a variety of services together. A key role played by many providers is recruiting a wide array of course producers and instructors to offer MOOCs through their respective course platforms. For example, Coursera forms partnerships with universities by offering a platform and support for their MOOC offerings, while also sharing a portion of any revenue generated through various services provided to course users.

Organizations acting as MOOC providers include both traditional nonprofit colleges and universities, such as MIT, Harvard, Stanford, and Yale, among others, but also for-profit start-ups such as Coursera, Udacity, and Udemy. Additionally, there are university-affiliated nonprofit entities, such as the MIT-Harvard partnership (later adding UC Berkeley and UT Austin) in the form of edX, which quickly became a major player in the MOOC arena. As I noted earlier, for-profit higher education institutions, including the likes of Capella, the University of Phoenix, and Walden University, are not part of this discussion because these entities do not generally offer online courses as open courses (for free or as shareable courses), which is a key aspect in the definition of a MOOC.[5] For obvious reasons, for-profits see little advantage in offering courses for free. This is not a criticism, just reality.

Early on, MIT was clearly the leader in advancing the idea of free and accessible course materials, through its MIT OCW initiative. By making such extensive and advanced course materials available to the world, MIT helped to open the door to the globalized MOOC movement, given that it was only a step away to take those same materials, provide some basic instructional support, and presto—a university course. Following the early creation of MIT OCW was the university's collaboration with Harvard, resulting in the 2012 formation of the nonprofit organization edX, which quickly became a leader in the nascent MOOC movement.

Prominent in the rise of the MOOC was the founding of private enterprises, with Coursera and Udacity leading the way. As was noted previously, nonprofit elite universities such as Columbia, Oxford, Stanford, and Yale explored the revenue-generating potential of online education in the form of Fathom and AllLearn and thus also helped to pave the way for the eventual rise of OCW and MOOCs. Indeed, the failures of Fathom and AllLearn in many ways taught higher education leaders, innovators, distance educators, and entrepreneurs valuable lessons. One important learning outcome was recognition of the lack of interest in fee-based online courses absent credentialing, even when offered by elite universities.

Building on the success of the Siemens-Downes original MOOC and then his own efforts at Stanford in offering a MOOC on artificial intelligence, computer scientist and roboticist Sebastian Thrun helped to co-found Udacity, selecting the company's name based on the goal of being "audacious, for you, the student," as Thrun's Stanford homepage claims.[6] The early mission of Udacity reflected democratic educational values, stressing the need to make higher education available to everybody around the world.

Another popular provider, Coursera, was founded by Stanford computer science professors Daphne Koller and Andrew Ng about the same time as Thrun's Udacity. Today, the company presents itself as "an education platform that partners with top universities and organizations worldwide, to offer courses online for anyone to take, for free." Coursera claims to "envision a future where everyone has access to a world-class education" and aims "to empower people with education that will improve their lives, the lives of their families, and the communities they live in."[7] The fact that Coursera and Udacity were founded as for-profits left many skeptical of their early emphasis on democratizing higher education.

The emergence of for-profits such as Coursera and Udacity created confusion early on in the MOOC movement; after all, aren't MOOCs supposed to be open and hence free? If the online courses are free, then how do for-profit providers intend to make money? Indeed, why were for-profit companies such as Coursera and Udacity so central to the early discussions about MOOCs and their potential to revolutionize higher education? I discuss this topic extensively later in this chapter, when I consider how a combination of public good and for-profit interests came together to help propel the MOOC movement. Suffice it to say for now that for-profits largely emerged to explore a variety of revenue-generating opportunities that entrepreneurs and educational innovators foresaw being linked to MOOCs, especially in light of growing participation in online education globally. In other words, although the actual course might be free, a host of other services could be linked to a MOOC, including credentialing in the form of course credit, badges, certificates, or degrees.

An example of the possibilities for credentialing are evident in Coursera's Signature Track program, which offers "verified" certificates to MOOC students in exchange for fees, generating revenue for both Coursera and its university partners (Kolowich 2014b). The Signature Track program uses software that recognizes keyboard signatures (the pattern of one's typing) to confirm the identity of students submitting their online course work, be that homework assignments, projects, quizzes, or exams. As Coursera explained in the company's blog: "Signature Track securely links your coursework to your identity, allowing you to confidently show the world what you've achieved on Coursera." The blog went on to note three basic benefits of Signature Track:

- *Identity Verification.* Offers an online user the chance to create a special profile linking her/his coursework to a real identity using a photo ID and the user's unique typing pattern.
- *Verified Certificates.* Offers online course completers "official recognition from universities and Coursera" for their accomplishments in the form of a "verifiable electronic certificate."
- *Shareable Course Records.* Offers electronic course records available for employers, educational institutions, or other entities "through a unique, secure URL."[8]

MOOC users who join Coursera's Signature Track program—for a fee of $30 to $100 per course in 2014—have course pass rates at about 70 percent, according to Koller (Kolowich 2013a). This is no small accomplishment.

Udacity also pursued the certificate idea as a possible revenue source and once offered four different types based on the level of academic performance: completion, distinction, high distinction, and highest distinction; edX offered certificates for completing some of its courses, bearing the edX logo along with the particular X-brand of the university offering the course, in the form of BerkeleyX, HarvardX, MITx, or UTAustinX ("Big Three" 2012). The awarding of certificates created another organizational role that partially was filled by Pearson VUE testing, adding another functional role—in the form of "legitimizing"—to the complexity of the emerging organizational system.

MOOC Legitimizers

As MOOC providers sought to develop creative strategies for generating revenue, a variety of entities came to play diverse supporting roles. For example, not only did for-profit companies such as Coursera and Udacity seek revenue-generating models, but so too did some of the nonprofit leaders, including Harvard and MIT. After all, even the wealthiest of U.S. universities have a difficult time committing $30 million to developing MOOCs, as Harvard and MIT did in January 2012, without getting a return on their investment. If MOOCs ultimately proved to be nothing more than service to the public good, as some seemed to believe they might be, recovering a percentage of costs was a reasonable goal. As a consequence of such concerns, increased interest emerged with regard to MOOCs and credentialing, mostly in the form of badges, certificates, and degrees.

To offer some form of a credential, MOOC providers such as edX, Coursera, Colorado State University, and University of the People (UoPeople), the latter offering associate's and bachelor's degrees in both business administration and computer science, needed methodologies for confirming student course completion and academic performance. Discussions proceeded with regard to ways of verifying that a MOOC participant met some minimal level of course competencies, as well as basic strategies for authenticating the identity of the actual course taker. Although Coursera mostly relied on the previously discussed Signature Track program, other providers turned to testing companies such as Pearson VUE, which at one time agreed to offer testing services for both edX and Udacity. Such services in most cases involved MOOC takers showing up at one of Pearson's four thousand worldwide testing centers to physically sit for a proctored exam. It is important to keep in mind here that choosing to pursue a credential necessitates either an exam or some type of verification procedure, such as Coursera's keystroke recognition system. Nick Anderson (2013), writing for the *Washington Post* based on an interview with Pearson president and CEO Robert Whelan, described the company's testing procedure: "A student registers in advance for a test and goes to a testing center. Pearson takes a digital photograph of the student, a palm-vein scan and a digital signature. Pearson asks for two forms of identification. At least two proctors observe the testing." Whelan stressed that Pearson digitally records "every single moment" a student is seated at a testing center. As a side note, Pearson had another angle to play in terms of MOOC revenue: The company also was involved in textbook publishing and, as *The Economist* noted, stood to benefit in multiple ways from its involvement with MOOCs ("Attack of the MOOCs" 2013).

Although Pearson as a MOOC legitimizer captures aspects as to why the for-profit sector sought to engage with the emergent MOOC movement, non-profit organizations also became involved in activities associated with legitimizing MOOCs. A key player early on was the American Council on Education (ACE), an organization representing presidents from U.S. accredited two- and four-year colleges and universities, including public and private, nonprofit and for-profit institutions. ACE already had a credit recommendation program, known as ACE CREDIT, established in 1974 for the purpose of assisting colleges and universities in offering course credit for workplace experience and nontraditional forms of learning. ACE's website notes that it has reviewed over 35,000 courses, making it a "national leader" in assessing education and training beyond the traditional college classroom.[9] When Coursera first submitted a request to ACE to review five MOOCs in 2012, the company had only been in business for one year. ACE's rules generally required an educational provider to have been operating for at least three years. But given that Coursera's courses represented a partnership of sorts with ACE member universities—namely, the University of California, Irvine, and Duke—ACE officials decided to waive this facet of their rules. In the end, all five Coursera courses earned a credit recommendation in the areas of science and mathematics; this meant that ACE viewed them as legitimate two- and three-credit college-level courses. However, this recommendation did not mean that a college or university must accept such courses for credit—ACE does not have such authority. What it meant was that ACE's faculty experts verified the legitimacy of the MOOCs as college courses. This was new ground for both the association and the MOOC movement. It also secured ACE as a key player in the role of legitimizing MOOCs for credit.

Funders

One of the most dramatic facets of the MOOC movement is the degree to which MOOCs captured the fancy of venture capitalists and individual investors. Indeed, it is hard to recall a recent educational innovation that so captured the interests of educationally minded investors, evidenced by the large support for MOOC-related start-up companies such as Coursera and Udacity. For example, the *Chronicle of Higher Education* ("Major Players" 2013) identified several such investors, including the following key players: Philippe Lemont, Jonathan Grayer (former chairman and CEO of Kaplan), Ann and John Doerr, Peter Levine, Andreessen Horowitz, New Enterprise Associates, and Kleiner Perkins Caufield and Byers. Andreessen Horowitz, for example, provided $15 million in start-up funds to Udacity. Perhaps the biggest coup of all was Coursera raising $43 million in investment capital from a group that included the World Bank. Such funding was likely to help the company expand globally, particularly into potentially lucrative markets such as China. In terms of venture capital firms, LearnCapital, a Silicon Valley firm, was a major contributor to Coursera.

Beyond the VCs and individual investors, foundations also played a significant role in financially supporting the MOOC movement, with four in particular taking the lead: the Bill and Melinda Gates Foundation, the William and Flora Hewlett Foundation, the Alfred P. Sloan Foundation, and the John D. and Catherine T. MacArthur Foundation. In addition to supporting educational exploration relative to MOOCs, these four foundations also helped to legitimize MOOCs as an educational innovation, lending their name and credibility to the movement.

The Gates Foundation allocated millions of dollars for the further development and advancement of MOOCs, including funds to edX to support course development and funds to ACE to further its credit review of MOOCs. The latter two are among a list of other development-oriented MOOC projects funded by the foundation. Gates also supported MOOC research, with one example being the MOOC Research Initiative (MRI). This project was developed to explore the potential of MOOCs to expand access to higher education credentials via more personalized and affordable pathways. The MRI was led by Siemens, initially when he was at Athabasca University in Canada and then later when he left for the University of Texas at Austin. The MRI included a grant competition focusing on innovative studies of MOOCs. In all, the MRI received seventy-nine full submissions for MOOC projects, with funding eventually allocated to twenty-eight proposed projects, including such topics as conceptualizing interaction and learning in MOOCs, peer assessment and academic achievement, characteristics and completion rates of MOOC participants, and social network formation in the context of MOOCs.[10] Another by-product of the MRI is the MOOC Research Hub, which serves as an online network and includes research papers and reports about open online education and open online courses. This research network offers an important vehicle for bringing diverse MOOC scholars and practitioners together to share ideas and results.

The Hewlett Foundation, beginning around 2002, has been a huge funder of the OER movement, and of course, OER helped lay the groundwork for the rise of OCW and MOOCs. A 2013 white paper from the Hewlett Foundation captured the critical role it played in support of OER and the eventual OCW movement:

> Since the Hewlett Foundation began investing in open educational resources in 2002, the field has blossomed from the seed of an idea into a global movement. In those early days, the Foundation recognized the revolution OER represented, and helped catalyze the movement by funding the Massachusetts Institute of Technology's online course project known as OpenCourseWare. (6)

Hewlett saw OER as key to addressing the growing worldwide demand for educational services, noting that by 2017 the Foundation "expects that OER will be increasingly integrated into the educational mainstream, improving the effectiveness of education at all levels throughout the United States and around the world" (12).

The Alfred P. Sloan Foundation, through the Sloan Consortium, also contributed to the MOOC movement both in terms of funding research and by supporting and organizing conferences about online education innovations, including most recently MOOCs (in this regard, the Sloan Consortium may also be considered as part of the networks and associations forming the MOOC organizational system to be discussed in the next section). For example, in recent years the consortium typically organized and funded three annual meetings focused on online education innovations, including an international conference. The consortium also supports the *Journal of Asynchronous Learning Networks*, which offers a venue for researchers studying innovations in online education.

The MacArthur Foundation also has an interest in open education and the growing role of digitized knowledge and computerized teaching and learning environments. A recent example is the Reclaim Open Learning Initiative, a collaboration with the Digital Media and Learning Research Hub at the University of California, Irvine and MIT Media Lab.[11] This initiative seeks to bring "together the best of truly open, online and networked learning in the wilds of the Internet." The foundation's interests mostly hinge on identifying the "kinds of innovations in pedagogy and online development" that enable and expand access "to meaningful and engaged forms of education for independent learners everywhere." Like Gates and Hewlett, the MacArthur Foundation sees forms of networked and open educational opportunities, made available by Internet-based technologies, in terms of their potential to further educational access. Furthermore, the MacArthur Foundation envisions such educational transformations as part of the solution to many of the challenges confronting twenty-first-century educational institutions.

Governmental agencies also put money into developing MOOCs as well as broader OER/OCW initiatives. The National Science Foundation (NSF) funded numerous research projects to assess the impact of MOOCs, giving, for example, $200,000 to MIT's Teaching and Learning Laboratory to study students enrolled in edX's famous circuits and electronics course. The project principle investigator, Lori Breslow, emerged as one of the leaders in assessing

MOOCs and their impact. The U.S. federal government is not alone, though, in supporting online educational innovations such as MOOCs. The European Union's European Commission has supported OER/OCW and MOOCS in significant ways, including launching Open Education Europa in 2013 as a single gateway for all European OER. China's government also began investing heavily in MOOCs. A case in point was their 2013 partnership with edX to develop the nation's own MOOC platform, XuetangX (*xuetang* or 学堂 means school in Chinese). The goal of this national platform was to work with a consortium of roughly a dozen Chinese universities, including the nation's two most prestigious universities—Peking and Tsinghua. China's embrace of MOOCs is hardly surprising given the nation's long-standing commitment to distance education and self-study, a strategy used for many years to reach remote parts of its vast geography.

Networks and Associations

A variety of networks and associations also emerged to offer support to the MOOC and OCW movements, including the aforementioned MRI and the subsequent MOOC Research Hub. The Research Hub offers a variety of resources, including reports from the Gates-sponsored MRI research projects and a regular blog led by Siemens. In addition to the MOOC Research Hub, another online site encouraging networking is MOOCs News and Reviews, self-described as an independent multiauthor blog. This is a useful site with MOOC-related articles and shorter posts, including a variety of resource-oriented discussions focusing on copyright issues, completion rates, professional development for teachers, and applying MOOC lessons to traditional classroom instruction. MOOCs News and Reviews also offers extensive analysis on a range of MOOCs. For example, a selection in June 2014 revealed discussions of the following MOOCs: "Introduction to Mathematical Philosophy" (Coursera), "ChinaX" (Harvard), "Introduction to Psychology" (Coursera), "Ancient Greek History" (Yale), and "Technology Entrepreneurship I" (NovoEd). I found the site to be quite useful in furthering knowledge of the overall MOOC movement and for better understanding the range of issues typically considered to be significant.

But earlier networks proved even more critical to strengthening OCW, including the OCW Consortium and the Community College Consortium for Open Educational Resources, among others. The OCW Consortium is a global network of hundreds of higher education institutions and associated organizations committed to expanding open education worldwide. The OCW Consortium reportedly seeks to solve the world's social problems by expanding access to education.[12] The mission of the Community College Consortium for OER is to expand "access to education by promoting awareness and adoption of Open Educational Resources."[13] As of March 2014, the consortium's website claimed that over two hundred colleges had joined the network.

In addition to the six aforementioned entities and social actors composing the MOOC organizational system, there are countless other entities contributing to the MOOC movement in both major and minor ways. Some play multiple roles, such as Google, which provides technical support, human capital, education-related software, investment capital, research funding, and so forth. Other organizations may not fit so easily within the categories delineated in this chapter, such as Khan Academy, which doesn't really develop MOOCs but does offer open course content potentially useful to MOOC developers, including digitally recorded lectures. I have no doubt that in the coming months new types of systemic roles are likely to emerge, especially as the movement continues to evolve and the organizational system undergirding it further expands both in terms of differentiation and reach. Future changes are likely to reflect a mix of both public good and private enterprise interests, given the important role both have played to this point.

Public Good and Private Interests in Support of MOOCs

An important facet to the emergence and expansion of MOOCs was the way in which both public good sentiments and the interests of private capital came together to support the movement. Indeed, the MOOC movement in many ways may be understood as a hybrid phenomenon of sorts—a mix of both public and private ambitions. Of course, this is not uncommon for higher education innovations in the United States, given that the industry is highly subsidized by tax dollars and yet orchestrated in significant ways by market-driven impulses, including stiff competition for students and faculty. At the heart of this marriage between public and private interests rests a basic question: Just what is it that a MOOC accomplishes?

Echoing the spirit of master architect Louis Kahn's famous question about the essence of design—"What does a brick want?"—Sherry Turkle (2009), in *Simulations and Its Discontents*, applied similar logic to better understanding the expanding role of simulation and design in science, asking: "What does simulation want?" (6). Applying this same thinking to the world of the MOOC, I pose this basic question: What does a MOOC want? Considering the problem of reification and the idea that a MOOC cannot "want," allow me to phrase this another way: What need does a MOOC address? Or more broadly speaking: What role do MOOCs play in the landscape of higher education? Addressing this latter question is a helpful starting point for better understanding the complex synergy between public good and private interests relative to shaping the MOOC movement.

So, what is the role of the MOOC? First, a MOOC is often framed as a modality for extending university-level courses to potential learners with limited access to higher education. This includes learners anywhere in the world. MOOCs thus are framed as a method for addressing inequities associated with higher education access, reflecting the idealistic conviction that everyone deserves access to a college education in some manner or form. This is consistent with UNESCO's (2000) vision of lifelong education as a key component of the expansion of rights to education for everyone. Such a perspective is widely embraced as part of a public good vision of higher education. Unfortunately, offering a brick-and-mortar college education to everyone is financially challenging, especially when demand is great and public support limited. The Hewlett Foundation's 2013 white paper on open educational resources captured part of the dilemma here: "In the United States and around the world, the demand for high quality education has never been greater. By 2025 there will be 263 million students who will be eligible for higher education. In order to accommodate this demand, at least 4 universities of 30,000 students would need to open every week for the next 15 years" (6). Obviously, the world is unlikely to keep pace with the demands for higher education. Hence, an early vision of the MOOC was that of helping to address the pressing demand for higher education; in essence, the MOOC was framed as a solution to a crisis of access.

A second possible response to questions about the role of the MOOC is more about fixing a common university problem—MOOCs may help address shortages of high-demand, lower-division courses and the related problem of students getting "locked out" of required courses. This happens quite often at community colleges and at four-year public universities, where course enrollment demands often exceed institutional capacity. I experience this problem at a personal level every fall when I teach an undergraduate course in the education studies minor at UCLA. Even though I recently expanded the course from forty to eighty students, for one reason or another many are unable to enroll in time and eventually get locked out. Unfortunately, due to limited classroom seats—the classroom in which I typically teach "only" holds eighty-one students—I cannot add them. Keep in mind that UCLA is not exactly the sort of under-resourced public university that typically comes to mind when considering these sorts of problems. Obviously, course shortages are likely to be more severe at community colleges and less resourced public universities.

The type of enrollment problem just described is of course tied to the reality that many public institutions operate with limited instructional funding and hence do the best they can with the means at their disposal. To put this in more concrete terms: If students at Underfunded State University (USU) have great difficulty getting into an overloaded and required algebra, English, or history course, but can take a similar online version in the form of a MOOC, then why shouldn't USU accept the free online course as a replacement for the overloaded one, assuming of course that their participation and learning outcomes are verifiable? Consider further that the free MOOC may actually be developed by a professor from Yale or MIT.

This take on the role of MOOCs pretty much reflected the stance of the California legislature in 2013, when it proposed SB-520 Student Instruction: California Online Student Incentive Grant Programs. SB-520 sought to require the president of the University of California, the chancellor of the California State University, and the chancellor of the California Community Colleges, "in consultation with their respective statewide academic senates, to each develop a list of 20 high-demand lower division courses . . . deemed necessary for program completion, deemed satisfactory for meeting general education requirements, or in areas defined as transferable lower division courses." The bill eventually was dropped when increasing questions were raised about MOOCs, especially after experimentation within the California State University resulted in "disappointing student performance," including widespread student failure (Rivard 2013b). Nonetheless, the potential to ameliorate overcrowding in lower-division courses is another of the apparent public good interests MOOCs may address. Of course, there are a number of criticisms one might offer here, and in fact in chapter 4 I offer several of my own. But for now suffice it to say that MOOCs were envisioned as a reasonable solution to overcrowded lower-level courses at financially strapped institutions.

Returning to Louis Kahn's famous question, when we think about what a brick wants, several purposes may come to mind. A brick may help to form the basic structure of a building, a new library perhaps; it may form a wall, protecting young children from straying onto the street. A brick can serve as a doorstop, to allow a gentle breeze to flow through a musty home on a humid summer night. But a brick can also be used for revolutionary purposes, such as when it is tossed through the window of an edifice linked to the ruling class, as Russian peasants did in 1917 during the early days of the Russian Revolution or as the Weathermen did as they ran through the streets of Chicago in 1969 during the "Days of Rage." A MOOC can also be used for revolutionary purposes, as a means of disrupting the status quo in academe. One might easily argue that this is the primary role of the MOOC. This revolutionary or transformative contribution may be interpreted as a form of public good in the sense that it disrupts stagnant colleges and universities too slow to adjust to the pressing needs of a higher education–hungry public. But this revolutionary facet of the MOOC also offers a glimpse into the interests of entrepreneurs and venture capitalists, who early on envisioned its disruptive force. In this regard, we might reasonably consider the MOOC as a vehicle for a variety of diverse players to further engage the higher education industry. After all, few services in today's increasingly knowledge-driven societies hold the revenue-generating potential of educational services.

What can we say then about how private interests came to shape the MOOC movement and intersect in important ways with public good concerns, such as those relating to issues of access? One obvious point to make in analyzing the early positioning of private interests was their rhetorical alignment with democratic concerns about access. Educational entrepreneurs and innovators spoke early and often of how MOOCs could further the democratization of higher education. They consistently expressed concerns about the fact that many potential students were denied access to meaningful learning opportunities. That they might adopt this discursive strategy is not too surprising. After all, would we really expect entrepreneurs and venture capitalists to openly acknowledge their intent to make a boatload of money off of an education-starved public? Mentioning profit taking in discussions about the democratization of higher education and the needs of low-income populations is likely to be perceived negatively. Can we really imagine venture capitalists, as smart as they are, being so crass as to say something along these lines: "Given the great demand for education globally, I want to get filthy rich offering marginal-income learners a highly scalable product that I can reproduce over and over on the cheap." Such comments are unlikely to take place in public venues, in front of foundation officers, or in the midst of progressive educators in the field of adult, lifelong, and distance education—many of the folks who originated the idea of the MOOC.

In raising critical questions about the role of private interests in advancing the MOOC movement, I am not suggesting that there is no place for venture capitalists and competitive, market-driven processes in helping to meet the pressing demands of mass higher education. Most have come to obligingly accept such realities in the face of decades of shifting educational policies evidenced to a great extent by increased marketization and privatization in both K-12 and higher education sectors (Apple 2000; Slaughter and Rhoades 2004). That MOOCs might be situated within the logic of marketization and privatization is not so surprising, and yet hard-core capitalists entering into the MOOC fray were astute enough to tread lightly, at least initially, by connecting their ambitions to the democratization-of-higher-education discourse.

All of this is to suggest that private interests played an important role in shaping the early MOOC movement. This assertion is most evident when examining the rise of key MOOC providers such as Coursera and Udacity and the amount of venture capital flowing into such start-up companies. But how did these for-profit enterprises position themselves, and what challenges did they face during the early days of the MOOC movement? Here, I find the case of Udacity most compelling.

Sebastian Thrun emerged on the higher education reform scene as a genius inventor, roboticist, Stanford research professor, and lead designer of Google's automated vehicle, known as Stanley. He received the prestigious Smithsonian Ingenuity Award in 2012 and the Max Planck Research Award in 2011. He was named by the online magazine *Fast Company* as one of the "Most Creative People" in 2011. *Forbes* included him as part of the "E-Gang," a list of seven technology leaders, in 2006. *Fortune* named him as one of the "Smartest People in Tech" in 2010. He is also a member of the National Academy of Engineering and the German Academy of Sciences. In my lifetime, I have seen few scholars as decorated as Thrun. With the success of his 2011 artificial intelligence MOOC ("Introduction to Artificial Intelligence"), co-taught with Peter Norvig, Thrun went on to found Udacity with David Stavens and Mike Sokolsky early in 2012. From the start Thrun made clear his commitment to democratizing higher education in the form of expanding access to courses, making full use of the MOOC model. The Udacity website described him as setting "his sights on democratizing higher education." In a 2012 keynote address titled "Democratizing Higher Education" delivered at the eighteenth annual Sloan

Consortium International Conference on Online Learning, he offered the following remarks, particularly addressing the mission of Udacity:

> The mission of the company is to make education available throughout the world to everybody. We actually believe just like many of you that education is a basic human right, it's the key enabler to prosperity, to personal growth, and to contributions to society. . . . I believe that higher education is in a bit of a crisis, so finding new innovative ways to be able to reach students and educate them should be front and foremost to all of us.

He went on to describe what he saw as the basic problem of higher education, defining it as a "problem of scale"; essentially, he argued that higher education must scale up to teach larger and larger numbers of students and in a manner that aligns pedagogy with massive online classrooms.

Despite Thrun's noble ambition, when Udacity teamed up with San Jose State University early in 2013 to develop and offer lower-level undergraduate courses in the form of MOOCs, including remedial math, the courses ultimately were described as a failure. "Udacity Project on Pause" was how it was described by Ry Rivard (2013b), writing for *Inside Higher Ed*. Rivard went on to report how SJSU provost Ellen Junn described disappointing student performance as a key factor in the university's decision to stop offering courses with Udacity as part of a "short breather." The *San Jose Mercury News* was less diplomatic, reporting that 56 to 76 percent of students failed final exams associated with five Udacity/SJSU courses covering the following subjects: elementary statistics, college algebra, entry-level math, introduction to programming, and introduction to psychology (Dearen 2013).

The setback presented Thrun's start-up with more than a bump in the road; it essentially represented a failed attempt by Udacity to gain a foothold into the mainstream higher education marketplace. With his inability to make inroads into the higher education industry, Thrun revealed great flexibility by quickly shifting gears and pivoting Udacity toward online corporate training. MOOCs suddenly seemed limited to Thrun as the basis of a higher education revenue model.

In light of his earlier grandiose claims to democratizing higher education, Thrun became vulnerable to widespread criticism, especially from bloggers who quickly jumped on Udacity's failed attempt, in the process making Thrun the poster child of "MOOCs gone wild." One higher education blogger, for example, had a field day with his shift in direction:

But what is the big deal about Thrun's pivot, and why are academics and higher-ed writers alternately wary and gleeful about it? On the surface, Thrun appears duly chagrinned that his brainchild, so proudly hailed in neoliberal wet dreams, has failed the tired, poor, and huddled masses yearning to learn for free. And on the surface, the new direction of Udacity, which is to leave the university environment and focus on corporate training courses, seems appropriate: Sure, go "disrupt" a bunch of corporations, they love that kind of thing. (Schuman 2013)

What became of his mission to democratize higher education? It seems online learning is not so profitable when the targeted users are, as the above blogger noted, "so damn poor."

The case of Udacity raises important issues about the organizational system that arose to support MOOCs and the coming together of public good motives and those driven more by profit taking. Was the democratization-of-higher-education discourse simply a rhetorical tool delivered by profit-seeking innovators presenting their wares in the context of the highly subsidized higher education marketplace?

Although Udacity raises a number of concerns about how for-profit interests could potentially be concealed by democratic rhetoric, Coursera seemingly took a different direction. There is evidence that Coursera shares a "public-spirited mission" with nonprofit universities, as Richard Levin, the former twenty-year president of Yale University, who took over as its chief executive in 2014, claimed. For example, when the MOOC road became increasingly bumpy with claims about MOOCs revolutionizing higher education dissipating, Coursera stayed the course, building a stronger and stronger portfolio of partners and course offerings. But the fact remained that Coursera was a for-profit company, and the start-up had raised over $65 million in investment capital by July 2013 (Korn 2013). As a for-profit entity, Coursera still needed to develop a consistent and viable revenue model. After all, a corporation, whether it has a vision of service to the public or not, still has one primary goal: maximizing profit, or at the very least turning a profit. Thus, as Udacity increasingly turned to corporate training opportunities, Coursera continued to consider possible revenue sources, furthering its desire to contribute to the democratic ideals of higher education access, but in a manner consistent with the priorities of a for-profit company. One obvious consideration, and consistent with naming Levin as CEO, was global markets, including China. This brings to mind the reality of the MOOC as a global phenomenon.

Global Facets of the MOOC Movement

Early on MOOCs revealed their global appeal with course takers coming from a wide range of countries and regions around the world. For instance, data from eighteen HarvardX courses revealed that 58 percent of users were from countries other than the United States (Nesterko et al. 2014). A study of six MOOCs offered by Edinburgh University (2013) in the United Kingdom, offered in conjunction with Coursera, showed that the vast majority of its course enrollees were international: only 11 percent were from the United Kingdom, while 89 percent were from other countries, with 28 percent from the United States. In addition to the global quality of MOOC users, providers (and various platforms as well) emerged around the world, including the likes of FutureLearn in the United Kingdom, iversity in Germany, Open2Study in Australia (affiliated with Open University, a long-time leader in distance education), Schoo in Japan, and Veduca in Brazil. The latter example, Veduca, had reached over 3 million users by January 2014 and secured VC funding totaling some $1.3 million, in part by aggressively offering MOOC completers certificates issued by the Brazilian Ministry of Education (Else 2014).

The international quality of MOOC users and the global facet of the movement in general partially explain Coursera's push to globalize and extend its operations aggressively in nations such as China. The hiring of Richard Levin as the company's new CEO in March 2014 was interpreted by some as further evidence of Coursera's commitment to expanding globally, especially in light of the fact that Levin had led Yale's liberal arts initiative in Singapore, in collaboration with National Singapore University. Steve Kolowich (2014b), writing for the *Chronicle of Higher Education*, assessed the company's decision: "Coursera . . . has been trying to expand in China. This past fall the MOOC provider announced a deal with NetEase, a Chinese Internet company, to build a Chinese-language portal for its courses, and it has been working with local universities and organizations in several countries to improve its offerings to non-English-speaking learners." Kolowich went on to add that Andrew Ng, cofounder of Coursera, hoped that Levin's business savvy and connections would help the company "grow in multiple target markets."

China obviously is an important market in the transnational higher education industry; the nation holds a special appeal to U.S.-based MOOC providers, given that Chinese students express great fondness for U.S. universities and their courses. The latter point is supported by data on international students studying in the United States; nearly one-third come from China. The actual figure for 2012–2013 was 287,260 Chinese students, amounting to twice the number from second-place India, which sent roughly 105,000 students (Newman 2014). In referencing the China market, Coursera's Eli Bildner, a member of Coursera's growth team, explained some of the company's emerging operations in China, including the creation of Coursera Zone: "Coursera and NetEase are joining together to create Coursera Zone—a NetEase-hosted, Chinese-language portal to Coursera.org. The aim in creating Coursera Zone is to help Chinese-speaking students more easily find and engage with content from Coursera's partner universities and institutions." When asked about why China is so important, Bildner responded, "We believe that hundreds of millions of people living in China stand to benefit from access to the free online courses offered by our partners. Today, however, a number of obstacles—from language to technical barriers—prevent Chinese students from taking full advantage of our resources."[14] Like Udacity, Coursera employs a discourse rooted in expanding access to higher education. Although Udacity came under great suspicion, especially after shifting to corporate training, the jury may still be out when it comes to Coursera's ultimate motives. The issue as to why Koller and Ng first chose a for-profit organizational structure rather than that of a nonprofit, following for instance the likes of Khan Academy, has come up before and is likely to arise again.

Making China a key target market, though, is a no-brainer. The possibilities seem endless, including potentially contributing to greater Internet openness, given that the entire operation may go nowhere if the Chinese government doesn't agree to some level of academic freedom in course content. As Levin noted in 2014 with regard to concerns about Internet censorship, Coursera does "not intend to get into the censorship business." However, he went to add that the company could not prevent a government from creating certain barriers to information (Kolowich 2014b). Barriers or not, China, with its vast population, a growing middle class, and thirst for U.S. higher education, offers significant revenue possibilities for Coursera, especially working in conjunction with its university partners.

The global quality of MOOCs is not surprising when one understands that the roots of the movement connect directly to the highly international OER movement. The international aspects of OER were captured by the Organisation for Economic Co-operation and Development (OECD) back in a 2007 report, *Giving Knowledge for Free: The Emergence of Open Educational Resources.* This report offered insight into the early stages of the OER/OCW movements, which of course helped to give rise to the MOOC. For example, the report highlighted the worldwide OER/OCW developments at the time, including the following (40):

- Worldwide, over 3,000 open access courses are were available from over 300 universities (these were not described as MOOCs at that time, but many would fit such a definition today).
- The United States offers approximately 1,700 open courses through various universities, including MIT, Rice, Johns Hopkins, Tufts, Carnegie Mellon, Notre Dame, and Utah State.
- China offers some 750 courses at 222 university members of the China Open Resources for Education (CORE) consortium.
- Japan has more than 400 courses available through the Japanese OCW Consortium.
- France has some 800 educational resources from around 100 teaching units affiliated with 11 member universities of the ParisTech OCW project.

The above OECD points are simply meant to offer a historical snapshot of an emerging global movement as it appeared in 2007. The power of OER ideals—grounded in the knowledge commons—has grown exponentially since then, providing the energy and foundation for the emergence of MOOCs. But as the movement expanded, gaining verve along the way, business-minded entrepreneurs took notice. So, while the OER/OCW movements grew from democratic ideals tied to making knowledge and information, including university courses, more accessible, others saw financial opportunities to develop revenue-generating models, especially with regard to the massive aspect of the MOOC. What resulted was a somewhat shifting landscape in which private interests came to influence the nature of the original public good ideals associated with the democratization of knowledge. With the rise of MOOCs, then, the goal of expanding college access (combined with the potential to generate profit) became an interest of private capital. Finally, the fact that OER, OCW, and MOOCs were global phenomena only strengthened their appeal to the imagination of educational innovators and entrepreneurs alike.

Concluding Thoughts

Admittedly, the organizational analysis in this chapter is a bit functionalist in orientation, but I see this as a necessary step given the newness of MOOCs and the challenge in making sense of a movement during what may very well be its formative years. Of course, bringing order to MOOCs through a systemic analysis is akin to systematizing chaos, or perhaps describing in detail the personality of a child at three years of age. Nonetheless, I have highlighted six key organizational entities, the coming together of both public and private interests, and the global quality of the overall MOOC movement. Although much is likely to change in the coming months and years, offering a glimpse into such a potentially important movement, at an early point in its development, has contemporary and historic benefits. At the very minimum, such analysis brings a degree of perspective to a complex and rapidly flowing phenomenon.

The organizational system of the MOOC is not in any way a planned or intentional entity; it is not a suburban housing development where every lot, every turn of a street, and every cul-de-sac is planned in advance. The organizational system of the MOOC arose rapidly from the fabric of existing organizations, including colleges and universities such as MIT and Harvard and private companies like Pearson VUE and Google. The rise of the MOOC also led to the creation of new organizational entities, including nonprofits such as University of the People and for-profits such as Coursera and Udacity. Traditional organizations also played a key role in the form of major foundations such as Gates, Hewlett, MacArthur, and Sloan. Governments too stimulated the growth of MOOCs, in the United States and around the world. Perhaps the most surprising facet of the organizational support of the MOOC was the role of venture capitalists and the huge funding they committed to start-up companies such as Coursera and Udacity.

3

Connectivism, Social Learning, and the cMOOC/xMOOC Distinction

In the previous chapter I focused on the organizational system that emerged to undergird the rise and development of the MOOC movement, including how both public good and private interests contributed to the growth of MOOCs. In a sense, my analysis extended outward beyond the actual phenomenon of the MOOC to examine and explain its organizational roots. In this chapter I turn more to the inner workings of MOOCs, most notably in terms of teaching and learning issues. More specifically, I argue that the age of the Internet has resulted in new ways of handling complex problems that increasingly involve collaborative problem-solving skills on the part of groups of thinkers and workers. Furthermore, group problem solving often is conducted in computer-mediated and Internet-based environments where taking advantage of collective intelligence becomes a necessity. Accordingly, new forms of teaching and learning based on connectivity, social learning, and collective intelligence are needed to complement more traditional forms mostly involving face-to-face interaction. The MOOC then may be understood as a form of innovation partially born from the need for more sophisticated teaching and learning strategies.

Within the MOOC movement, there emerged a divide of sorts between two divergent models: cMOOCs and xMOOCs (Haber 2014). On the one hand, cMOOCs stressed the original connectivist ideals of George Siemens and Stephen Downes, typically ignoring the credentialing aspects of the higher education enterprise. In a very real sense, they represented the purist ideals of adult learning—learning for learning's sake. The xMOOC, on the other hand, was more tied to the existing model of the university course, often framed as an "extension" of an existing course. Additionally, xMOOCs typically remained tied to the credentialing role of higher education. As I elaborate throughout this chapter, these differences are significant and must be examined to appreciate the complexity of the overall MOOC movement.

In terms of the overall objectives of the book, this chapter primarily addresses thesis 3, concerning the important distinction between cMOOCs and xMOOCs, and thesis 4, focused on the dominance of the xMOOC model and the need for further analysis. As I argue in this and the next chapter, if xMOOCs are to play a role in addressing challenges associated with expanding college access, then a better understanding of their strengths and weaknesses is needed.

As a starting point for framing this chapter, I find it helpful to briefly reiterate a key point from chapter 1: Significant technological changes to the World Wide Web resulted in new capabilities that came to be known as "Web 2.0." Here the work of Tim O'Reilly, founder of O'Reilly Media and one of the world's leading advocates of the open source movement, is insightful. His classic article "What Is Web 2.0?" (2006) is a key guide to explaining the transformation. O'Reilly envisioned Web 2.0 "as a set of principles and practices that tie together a veritable solar system of sites that demonstrate some or all of those principles at a varying distance from the core" (2). He went on to point out that a central principle of the so-called Internet giants, such as Hyperlinking, Yahoo, Google, eBay, and Amazon, born of Web 1.0 technologies but leading the way to 2.0, was their ability to embrace "the power of the Web to harness collective intelligence" (6). As he explained, "Much as synapses form in the brain, with associations becoming stronger through repetition or intensity, the web of connections grows organically as an output of the collective activity of all web users" (6–7). O'Reilly went on to highlight one of the classic examples of Web 2.0 collective intelligence, Wikipedia, which he described as "a radical experiment in trust" based on what seemed at one time like an "unlikely notion": that any Web user could create an entry and other users in turn could edit it. The logic, as he argued, was based on the thinking of a leading advocate in the open source software movement, Eric Raymond, and his classic dictum that "with enough eyeballs, all bugs are shallow," an idea originally applied to open source software (7–8).

The changes described by O'Reilly quickly migrated to the world of online education, making possible new and more complex ways for teachers and learners, producers and users (or produsers) to interact as collaborative learning communities, taking advantage of collective understanding and knowledge, or what he and others defined as collective intelligence. The increasing complexity associated with Web 2.0 capacities thus changed the way people interacted and altered how individuals saw themselves relative to others and relative to the new social worlds they could now inhabit. In this sense, the role of the Internet in people's lives fundamentally altered the way we live, not just relative to online courses such as MOOCs but in terms of our overall experiences with the social world. Because this social transformation is so critical to understanding how MOOCs quickly became reasonable educational alternatives, it is helpful to further explore the impact of the Internet on people's lives more broadly.

Connectivity and Simulation in the Age of the Internet

As the Internet came to play a larger role in the lives of significant populations of people, scholars began asking critical questions about how the nature of human experience might be changing. Was it possible that Internet-based interactions, indeed, Internet-based versions of reality, or hyper-reality as it came to be called, could somehow alter the human condition? Such questions particularly arose in light of the increasing engagement of young people with the Internet. The Internet made it possible for users to connect with greater numbers of people and in turn experience a form of connectivity previously unimagined. Even forms of mental illness were equated with Internet use or overuse, such as Internet addiction.

In her book *Alone Together*, Sherry Turkle (2011) discussed how the Internet initially served a functional role as a means for quick and easy communications but changed over time. She elaborated on this perspective:

> Online communications were first conceived as a substitute for face-to-face contact, when the latter was for some reason impractical: Don't have time to make a phone call? Shoot off a text message. But very quickly, the text message became the connection of choice. We discovered the network—the world of connectivity—to be uniquely suited for the overworked and overscheduled life it makes possible. And now we look to the network to defend us against loneliness even as we use it to control the intensity of our connections. Technology makes it easy to communicate when we wish and to disengage at will. (13)

This theme of technology-based connectivity and its impact on human interaction is of course a central quality to Turkle's work, going back to her earlier book *Life on the Screen* (1995), where she explored how identities may actually be influenced by engagement in various Internet-based interactive spaces, including identity exploration and role playing in multi-user domains (MUDs). A passage from *Life on the Screen* captures this point of view: "As more people spend more time in these virtual spaces, some go so far as to challenge the idea of giving any priority to RL [real life] at all" (14). She used some comments from a research subject, a dedicated MUD player, to reinforce her point: "After all, why grant such superior status to the self that has the body when the selves that don't have bodies are able to have different kinds of experiences" (14). Internet-based simulations and virtuality clearly were giving new meaning to "lived experience." Qualitatively oriented social scientists acknowledged as much in advancing new methodologies to examine online lived experience in the form of netnography and cyber-ethnography (Keeley-Browne 2011; Kozinets 2010). Such methodologies became useful for examining the world of the MOOC as well (Toven-Lindsey, Rhoads, and Berdan Lozano 2015).

In *Simulation and Its Discontents*, Turkle (2009) examined the age of computer design and simulation, pointing to basic social concerns, particularly noting what she described as overreliance on technology in the form of simulations of real life. She argued that scientific design and inquiry might suffer negative consequences if simulations were used uncritically and if there were a lack of transparency in the sophisticated programs scientists use to explore complex phenomenon. By "transparency," she referred to the ability to understand the workings behind particular programs. As she noted, "Transparency once meant being able to 'open the hood' to see how things worked. Now, with the Macintosh meaning of transparency dominant in the computer culture it means quite the opposite: being able to use a program without *knowing* how it works" (44). Part of her argument concerned differences between "old-school" professors possessing the ability to "open the hood" and a younger generation of students, scholars, and scientists more accepting of the complicated workings and "unknowns" of high technology. As she argued, "An older generation, one might say, is trying to get a younger to value experiences they never had and understand a language they never spoke" (44).

For Turkle, younger scholars tend to recognize the multilayered complexities of the contemporary engineered world; in order to make progress toward achieving the goals of any particular project, they see the need for an individual to at times trust in the knowledge of others. In this manner, a team of engineers—or simply a team of thinkers—can accomplish something far greater than that of any one individual. This type of work environment, or learning context, where one is dependent to a certain extent on the group's ability has been described as connectivity; in terms of a theory of teaching and learning, it is often discussed as connectivism.

Connectivity brings multiple thinkers together, potentially solving separate facets of a larger complex process. This involves an element of acceptance—acceptance of what one may not have time to understand or know, including how particular software functions or perhaps the significance of a specific facet of the human experience. In a world characterized by connectivity, where the advance of ideas, projects, and complex group endeavors may take place amidst an Internet-based knowledge community taking full advantage of collective intelligence, there is something an individual must give up in terms of seeing or experiencing the complete process, the full discovery. This seems inescapable and is arguably desirable in the face of gains associated with collective understanding. Although one might raise legitimate questions about what may be lost in a world of Internet-based specialists—an important concern stressed by Turkle—advanced research and development increasingly involves connecting online and working in simulated environments. This sort of thinking about collective intelligence and Internet-based connectivity helped to frame the early educational experiments giving rise to the MOOC.

Connectivist Learning Theory

The early MOOC phenomenon was tied to a group of learning-oriented educationalists who subscribed to the idea that the world is best understood as a complex networked environment in which significant social or physical problems can be solved only by groups of people working together. From such a perspective, the goal is to take advantage of each individual's expertise by building group-based solutions. This new theory of learning, connectivist learning theory, played a major role in framing the development of the first MOOCs.

The influence of the Internet on social life during the early part of the twenty-first century is critical to understanding the MOOC movement. Siemens (2004) was one of the first to talk about connectivist learning, using such a term in relation to the increasingly social aspect of learning in online communities. In advancing a connectivist perspective, Siemens identified several key learning trends:

- Learners are increasingly likely to move into a variety of different, possibly unrelated fields over the course of their lifetime.
- Informal learning is a significant aspect of the learning experience. Formal education no longer constitutes the majority of learning. Learning now occurs in a variety of ways—through communities of practice, personal networks, and work-related tasks.

- Learning is a continual process, lasting for a lifetime. Learning and work-related activities are interwoven, and in many situations they are one and the same.
- Technology is altering, perhaps rewiring, our brains, given that the tools people use define and shape the ways in which they think.
- Organizations, like individuals, have become learning organisms; accordingly, there is great need for theories that explain the links between individual and organizational learning.
- Many of the common processes of knowledge acquisition and performance, previously explained by basic learning theories, can now be performed by different forms of technology.
- Knowing *how* and knowing *what* are being supplemented with knowing *where* to find knowledge.

These key trends touch upon the increasingly complex, interconnected, and continuously changing nature of social life and learning in the contemporary age. At the heart of these trends is technology in general and the Internet in particular, which promote multiple ways for a wide range of learners to engage courses and materials in what Valerie Irvine described as "multi-access learning environments," meaning that prospective learners may access a course and its materials through a variety of channels, including face-to-face, online, or hybrid formats (Irvine 2009; Irvine, Code, and Richards 2013).

Undergirding changes in teaching and learning processes characterized by connectivism and social learning are what Siemens (2004) described as three primary epistemological traditions: objectivism, pragmatism, and interpretivism. He further argued that all of these are lacking in a world characterized by connectivity and social learning. Objectivism represents a view of learning in which knowledge and truth exist external to the knower; learning involves gaining knowledge through experience in the world. Objectivism as an epistemology is consistent with a behaviorist view of learning, in "that learning is largely unknowable" (the "black box theory"), with Siemens explaining, "We can't possibly understand what goes on inside a person." Pragmatism leads to what Siemens described as cognitivist explanations of learning: "Cognitivism often takes a computer information processing model. Learning is viewed as a process of inputs, managed in short term memory, and coded for long-term recall." From the perspective of cognitivism, to understand how people learn is to understand how their brains are wired and rewired. Both behaviorism and cognitivism "view knowledge as external to the learner and the learning process as the act of internalizing knowledge." The third epistemology delineated by Siemens is interpretivism, which he associates with constructivist forms of learning. This perspective stresses that reality is internal and that truth and knowledge are socially constructed. Although the constructivist perspective at least suggests the importance of community—in that knowledge is socially constructed through interactions with others—Siemens argued that it still situates knowledge as something an individual ultimately might possess, even though it may be formulated socially.

For Siemens, the Internet serves as a disruptive force in terms of how one views learning, given that people now exist in an environment in which information and knowledge are so abundant that they need particular skills for rapidly determining whether a particular body of knowledge is valuable or not. Plus, bodies of knowledge or information are constantly changing, and relying on our own brains to store and retrieve knowledge appears to be less relevant. As Siemens (2004) posited, "Additional concerns arise from the rapid increase in information. In today's environment, action is often needed without personal learning—that is, we need to act by drawing information outside of our primary knowledge." This led him to emphasize "the ability to synthesize and recognize connections and patterns" as a critical skill in a highly networked world.

Connectivism is based on a view that knowledge is dynamic and that people are bombarded by too much information. The contemporary world involves the ability to decipher and process knowledge and information rapidly, skills that arguably have not been at the center of previous models of learning. The ability to distinguish between important and unimportant information becomes a necessity in networked, hyper-connected environments. Such a world requires the ability to recognize that new knowledge may enter into the picture at any moment, thus requiring constant reassessment of previously drawn conclusions. These conditions led Siemens (2004) to delineate the basic principles of a new theory of learning, what he described as connectivist learning theory (4):

- Learning and knowledge rests in diversity of opinions.
- Learning is a process of connecting specialized nodes or information sources.
- Learning may reside in nonhuman appliances.
- Capacity to know more is more critical than what is currently known.

- Nurturing and maintaining connections facilitates continual learning.
- Ability to see connections between fields, ideas, and concepts is a core skill.
- Currency, or keeping up with knowledge, is the goal of connectivist learning activities.
- Decision making is a learning process. Choosing what to learn and the meaning of new information is seen through the lens of a shifting context. Answers are tentative in that what is correct one day may be incorrect the next, given the potential for information and conditions to change.

These principles offer the basics to a theory of learning that remains rather underdeveloped. But a key contribution Siemens made was in considering more concretely the role of networks in advancing collective understanding or collective intelligence.

Given the importance of collective intelligence, understanding the operation and role of social networks becomes increasingly important in the world of individual and organizational learning. This includes recognizing the role of hubs—well-connected people through whom information flows—in supporting other individual learners and the exchange of information throughout the larger organization. Of course, this kind of analysis has become increasingly popular, in part influenced by Mark Granovetter's (1973, 1983) work on network theory, including his conceptualizations of weak and strong ties, and then later as a result of the growth of social network analysis (SNA). Although the starting point for networked activity is largely the individual for Siemens (2004), the cycle of knowledge development takes place as flows of information among individuals, networks, and organizations, allowing "learners to remain current in their field through the connections they have formed." Siemens concluded by noting that the "amplification of learning, knowledge and understanding through the extension of a personal network is the epitome of connectivism." The basic principles of connectivism, as laid out by Siemens and others, are at the heart of what are described as connectivist MOOCs or cMOOCs.

Downes, co-instructor with Siemens of the first MOOC, also contributed significantly to advancing connectivism as a theory of learning. For example, in his oft-cited article published with the *Huffington Post* (2011) titled "'Connectivism' and Connective Knowledge," he drew comparisons between the brain and the sort of connections people now forge as part of Internet-based learning:

> What we learn, what we know—these are literally the connections we form between neurons as a result of experience. The brain is composed of 100 billion neurons, and these form some 100 trillion connections and it is these connections that constitute everything we know, everything we believe, everything we imagine. And while it is convenient to *talk* as though knowledge and beliefs are composed of sentences and concepts that we somehow acquire and store, it is *more accurate*—and pedagogically more useful—to treat learning as the formation of connections.

Downes suggested that learning itself in some ways needs to mirror the operations of the brain, as learners form connections almost continuously with the Internet serving as a quick and accessible vehicle for exploring the universe. He further maintained that "Knowledge is distributed across a network of connections, and therefore that learning consists of the ability to construct and traverse those networks."

Criticism has surfaced with regard to connectivist learning theory. At one level, the advocates of connectivism suggest that an individual learner does not need to know anything these days—all she or he needs is a lot of connections to other people (i.e., weak ties and strong ties) who presumably may know "things" or know how to find "things." It seems as though connectivist learning advocates at times confound knowledge and information, claiming that all one needs to do is access the proper nodes of an expansive network of information storage units in order to be knowledgeable. Study after study seeks to track the social networks of various individuals and groups. Colorful network diagrams often are included, depicting the many points and lines, the nodes and ties, representing the complex array of social linkages and interactions. Indeed, studies of MOOCs have used such methodologies to examine and then convey the extent of interactions during various structured activities, such as when enrollees are invited to participate in a Moodle discussion (Kop, Fournier, and Mak 2011). The degree to which connectivist learning theories situate networked connections as the end-all of knowledge acquisition should be further considered if this theory is to take root in more significant ways. It seems to me that knowledge is something quite different from information and that the individual mind is still quite critical to advancing knowledge.

As a professor who has worked with countless doctoral students over the past twenty years or so, I have observed an interesting phenomenon. The vast majority of the students with whom I work are in their mid to late twenties, with most having some modest professional experience. They are no doubt part of a generation of young scholars much more at ease with technology than I am; indeed, I might be considered a dinosaur by comparison. Given their more advanced technology skills and comfort with online communications, why then am I so much better at surfing the Internet for research-related ideas, concepts, and references? They mostly stumble onto things after days or weeks of searching, while I can find the same information literally in minutes. Perhaps there is a lesson here. Knowledge is more than simply the networks we access—it also involves an element of experience or wisdom that bears on both the search and formation of networks. It seems to me that a priori knowledge—conceptually-based understanding—is critical in helping learners recognize the value of particular nodes and ties. Also, a priori knowledge is useful in framing questions as part of conducting an online search. In short, there is more to knowledge acquisition than simply accessing networked information. I intend to say more about this in chapter 4 when I offer a more critical assessment of the MOOC movement, but for now it is instructive to keep such criticism in mind as part of further exploring differences between cMOOCs and xMOOCs.

cMOOCs and xMOOCs

The principles of connectivism undergird most of the more advanced MOOCs, which are described by some as cMOOCs, with the small "c" depicting "connectivist" qualities (Siemens 2013). The "x," according to Downes, refers primarily to the idea of "extension" or "extended" MOOCs, as in "extending" something into another arena. For instance, MIT extends beyond the local physical campus in the form of MITx.[1] Thus, the small "x" indicates that a program or course is an extended version of something else, typically a face-to-face course offered as part of a brick-and-mortar campus (hence, xMOOCs are also described as "institutionalized" MOOCs). What this suggests is that courses typically offered at a university as part of its regular curriculum may be described as xMOOCs when offered online for *free*.[2] Although xMOOCs as the more institutionalized version of the MOOC do not typically make use of connectivist forms of teaching and learning, this is not to suggest that they cannot; the problem is that connectivist modalities become increasingly difficult to implement as enrollment expands, and xMOOCs place great emphasis on scalability.

Another important distinction often made between cMOOCs and xMOOCs is the degree to which they reflect the ideals of the knowledge commons. For example, many MOOCs offered through providers such as Coursera or Udacity require course enrollees to agree to certain restrictions concerning the use of course-related materials. This by and large is done to provide copyright protections for the course materials produced by the university, company, or course designers, the latter typically being faculty members employed at a university. cMOOCs, though, tend to reflect the openness ideals of the OER/OCW movements and in fact are likely to encourage reusing, remixing, and reproducing materials for the benefit of a particular knowledge community. In this regard, cMOOCs are deeply tied to the value orientation of the knowledge commons—a perspective somewhat in opposition with that of traditional copyright norms. This is no small difference both philosophically and practically speaking.

Both cMOOCs and xMOOCs may rely on social learning and to varying extents connectivist learning principles, but cMOOCs tend to be less structured initially, less controlled pedagogically, and often less tied to an institutional home. One might think of the instructor-led MOOCs offered by course providers such as edX and Coursera as xMOOCs, whereas the type of MOOC initially taught by Siemens and Downes, wherein the community of learners was encouraged to further design and advance the course, is a classic example of a cMOOC. I tend to think of cMOOCs as more grassroots in nature, less formalized, less oriented toward credentials, and more in line with adult and lifelong learning ideals. I see xMOOCs as more institutionally situated and holding the potential to be applied toward forms of credentialing, be that a badge, certificate, or degree. The distinction made here should not be seen as a hard-and-fast rule but instead as a guide to unraveling a complicated and evolving landscape. Again, some xMOOCs—though certainly not the majority—may employ sophisticated methodologies for promoting connectivist learning.

Rita Kop (2011) offered insight into differences between MOOCs taught based on principles of direct instruction (traditional teacher-to-student instruction) versus MOOCs taught in a manner consistent with connectivist principles, such as the original Siemens-Downes course. For Kop, connectivist-based MOOCs, or cMOOCs, involve greater emphasis on self-directed learning and rely more heavily on social networks as sources of support for knowledge exploration and acquisition. She in fact used the term "networked learning" to capture the emphasis on self-directed exploration through countless Internet-based connections. She also noted that for such forms of learning to be most successful, a certain degree of "critical literacy" is needed, in terms of understanding the structure and basis of Internet content. As she maintained, "For networked learning to be successful, people need to have the ability to direct their own learning and to have a level of critical literacies that will ensure they are confident at negotiating the Web in order to engage, participate, and get involved with learning activities" (34). Critical literacy for Kop suggests certain abilities to not only access networked resources but to interrogate issues of power relative to the content. Such critical processes are likely to involve raising questions about what is included or excluded among content and who is represented or not represented. I elaborate on these and a host of other critical issues in chapter 4.

A key aspect of the cMOOC idea is that formal instructors should no longer be positioned as the only knowledge experts capable of assisting learners in developing and advancing their understanding. This disruptive quality of cMOOCs is pivotal. Kop, Helene Fournier, and John Sui Fai Mak (2011) explained it this way: "Emergent technologies provide different models and structures to support learning. They disrupt the notion that learning should be controlled by educators and educational institutions as information and 'knowledgeable others' are readily available on online networks through the press of a button for anyone interested in expanding his or her horizon" (75). Along these lines, Osvaldo Rodriguez (2012) noted that a marker of cMOOCs is the emphasis on course content and materials ultimately being "defined by participants" as courses progress rather than being developed by an instructor prior to the course starting (4). This flexibility on the part of the user or learner constitutes a key aspect of the "openness" in cMOOCs, especially when compared to xMOOCs (Rodriguez 2013).

At one level, there is clearly a democratic facet to the teaching and learning models supported by cMOOC advocates; in fact, at times their educational philosophy seems in line with Paulo Freire's (1970) critique of one-directional authoritarian forms of education and his advocacy for education as a dialogical process stressing active participation by students in creating knowledge. Again, Kop (2011) is insightful: "Connectivists advocate a learning organization whereby there is not a body of knowledge to be transferred from educator to learner and where learning does not take place in a single environment; instead, knowledge is distributed across the Web, and people's engagement with it constitutes learning" (20). What is lacking, though—and Kop addresses this ever so slightly—is a thorough critique of the ways in which power and capital may actually infect the Internet and the forms of knowledge and information available.

Active learning is a foundational element to cMOOCs, as advocated by early practitioner-scholars such as Dave Cormier and Siemens. For example, in their article "Through the Open Door," published in *EDUCAUSE Review*, Cormier and Siemens (2010) highlighted the active role learners are expected to assume in connectivist-oriented MOOCs:

> Regardless of how learners self-organize, the social contract in open courses differs from that in traditional courses. The social contract in an open course is based on the participatory pedagogy model. The educator provides a frame, foundation, or platform for learning through starting-point readings and resources. With this structure in place, learners are expected to actively contribute to the formation of the curriculum through conversations, discussions, and interactions. (36)

This type of social contract and related expectations tend to work well for MOOCs oriented toward professionals with a certain level of extant knowledge who are highly self-motivated, such as those in a professional community of practice. What is less clear is whether cMOOCs are likely to be successful in addressing more traditional college-going populations.

Building on the work of Downes (2011), Carol Yeager, Betty Hurley-Dasgupta, and Catherine Bliss (2013) argued that four activities are at the core of cMOOCs: aggregation or curation, involving an initial list of resources at a course website that then is further developed on a regular basis; remixing, which involves strengthening and refashioning connections through blogging, social bookmarking, or tweeting; repurposing, which involves users creating their own internal connections based on their learning experiences; and feeding forward, which involves sharing new connections. Downes previously highlighted these four essential ingredients in his *Huffington Post* article. Here, we begin to see more clearly the subtle differences in course design between cMOOCs and xMOOCs. On the one hand, cMOOCs encourage learners to actively remix and repurpose course material, information, and knowledge—to essentially direct their own learning experience and potentially influence a larger community of online learners. Ideally speaking, in cMOOCs the learner also becomes the teacher at times. On the other hand, although xMOOCs also encourage a certain degree of self-directed learning and learners may assist other online learners in knowledge exploration and acquisition, instructors are less likely to give up their role as course guides and facilitators. In other words, in xMOOCs the course instructor typically does not encourage individual students or groups of learners to redirect the course in significant ways. The structure of the xMOOC—especially considering that learners may have plans to seek course credit, often through a third party—is not so amenable to alterations. This is not intended as a criticism of xMOOCs but instead is simply noted as part of reaching a more nuanced understanding of the range of learning opportunities represented by cMOOCs and xMOOCs. Regardless of whether one is referencing cMOOCs or xMOOCs, online forms of social learning are at the heart of the MOOC movement.

Social Learning and MOOCs

The "c" and "x" are helpful in differentiating basic qualities between two major categories of MOOCs. Adding to their relevance is the fact that copyright issues and ideals relating to openness (e.g., the knowledge commons) may be quite significant in differentiating cMOOCs (which tend to stress openness) and xMOOCs (which are often more restrictive). Despite their differences, however, it is important to recognize that xMOOCs too may embrace social learning as a strategy and operate to a certain extent on principles of connectivism (this of course adds to the confusion). Given the reality that both cMOOCs and xMOOCs may embrace a broad array of social learning strategies, it is important to further examine social learning and its relevance to the world of the MOOC.

John Seely Brown and Richard Alder offered a rich discussion of social learning relative to the online education context, arguing that "social learning is based on the premise that our *understanding* of content is socially constructed through conversations about that content and through grounded interactions, especially with others, around problems or actions. The focus is not so much on *what* we are learning but on *how* we are learning" (2008, 18). They went on to contrast social learning with a more traditional view anchored in Cartesian sensibilities:

> The emphasis on social learning stands in sharp contrast to the traditional Cartesian view of knowledge and learning—a view that has largely dominated the way education has been structured for over one hundred years. The Cartesian

perspective assumes that knowledge is a kind of substance and that pedagogy concerns the best way to transfer this substance from teachers to students. By contrast, instead of starting from the Cartesian premise of *"I think, therefore I am,"* and from the assumption that knowledge is something that is transferred to the student via various pedagogical strategies, the social view of learning says, *"We participate, therefore we are."*

Clearly, a key element of the social learning model advanced by MOOC advocates is the active engagement of the learner in the acquisition and creation of knowledge. This view of social learning connects to the more democratic yearnings often expressed by constructivist educational theorists.

Social learning involves actively participating with other learners to advance knowledge acquisition, whether through identifying existing forms of knowledge or creating new understandings (Couros 2009). But what does this actually look like in the context of a MOOC? Here, it may be helpful to return to the source, the first MOOC designed and taught by Siemens, while at Athabasca University, and Downes, working for the National Research Council of Canada.

The Siemens-Downes MOOC focused on connectivist knowledge and incorporated several vehicles for promoting social learning: threaded discussions using Moodle, blog posts, and Second Life, a 3-D world where every character represents a real person participating in synchronous online meetings (Yeager et al. 2013, 134). Many MOOCs adopt these and other methods for fostering social engagement by promoting the development of online learning communities.

Rodriguez (2012) analyzed several MOOCS offered in Belgium, Canada, and the United States, noting in particular some of the cMOOC facets, suggesting that they are "multispaced courses where the learner's blogs and personal spaces define much of the learning" (2). He also identified particular courses and the social learning strategies employed. Rodriguez described tools used in the MOOCs he analyzed: mailing lists with frequent email messages; a Moodle site with a wiki-style page; Elluminate (a synchronous Web conferencing system); Ustream (a video streaming system); Pageflakes and Netvibes (services that allow aggregation of rich site summary or RSS feeds); Facebook; LinkedIn; Twitter; Ning (a service that allows users to create their own personalized social networks); Second Life; Twine (a semantic Web service for collecting and connecting content by topic); Flickr (a popular photo sharing service); social bookmarking (a generic term for services that allow users to store and share bookmarks); and Web tools to collaboratively edit conceptual and mental maps (7). Other social learning tools such as gRSShopper, a Web environment enabling resource aggregation, have been used by MOOC designers to encourage better organization of user-produced content like commentary on discussion boards. All of the aforementioned add to the potential of MOOCs to encourage the kind of distributed learning (not centered in one physical space or with one individual) made possible by 2.0 technologies. However, it should be kept in mind that the kinds of experiences (and learning outcomes) students have in diverse social learning environments fostered by MOOCs are likely to vary on the basis of student motivation and preferences as well as on the basis of the type of social media deployed (Eynon 2014).

The aforementioned tools offer the potential to promote forms of social learning by encouraging learners to work and communicate in online learning communities, to provide feedback about ideas and creative content (e.g., term papers, conceptual maps, photos, etc.), and to develop content and projects through interactive group processes. These types of learning experiences reflect advances associated with Web 2.0 and the connectivist principles undergirding cMOOCs. There is just one big problem—these sort of rich connectivist-oriented teaching and learning strategies are the exception and not the rule. The vast majority of MOOCs involve few opportunities for extensive social learning based on the ideals of connectivism; this is part of the reality—and challenge—of making a course massively open.

Rodriguez (2012) noted a difference between connectivist-oriented MOOCs such as those offered by Siemens and Downes by comparison to Stanford's CS221 "Introduction to Artificial Intelligence" (simply known as AI-Stanford) offered by Sebastian Thrun and Peter Norvig. The AI-Stanford course attracted roughly 160,000 enrollees, with about 20,000 actually completing the coursework. In addition to the Siemens-Downes MOOC, Rodriguez analyzed the following connectivist-oriented MOOCs: (1) PLENK2010, "Personal Learning Environments, Networks, and Knowledge" (with more than 1,600 participants by the final day), organized by the Technology Enhanced Knowledge Research Institute (TEKRI) at Athabasca University and offered by Siemens, Downes, Cormier, and Kop, a "who's who" in the world of online education innovation; (2) MobiMOOC, a six-week course with 556 participants offered in April 2011 by Ingatia de Waard from the Institute of Tropical Medicine (ITM) in Belgium and focused on mobile learning (mLearning);

and (3) EduMOOC, an eight-week course with 2,700 registered participants focused on "Online Learning Today . . . and Tomorrow," delivered from June to August 2011 by Ray Schroeder, professor emeritus and director of the Center for Online Learning, Research and Service at the University of Illinois, Springfield.

As a result of his analysis of differences in pedagogy (and the underlying theory of learning), Rodriguez noted that although the four aforementioned cMOOCs evidenced forms of social learning consistent with connectivist learning ideals, the AI-Stanford course was much more conventional in its pedagogical approach and in the theory of learning upon which it built, falling more in line with a cognitive-behaviorist approach. The AI-Stanford course represented an institutionalized attempt to scale up using a variety of MOOC-like practices but failed to capture the full social learning potential associated with connectivist MOOCs. Massive scale-up may necessitate compromising the best teaching and learning practices associated with connectivist ideals and the development of rich social learning environments. Rodriguez went on to posit that the AI-Stanford course is suggestive of an online educational format different from the connectivist-oriented MOOC, in that "AI essentially gives the traditional course a digital facelift" (12), but remains anchored in a limited view of teaching and learning. Rodriguez concluded that institutionalized efforts by the likes of Coursera and edX tend to represent an effort to "transfer" a traditional course to an online platform (in the form of an xMOOC), rather than to "transform" the course in a manner consistent with the social learning practices of the connectivist teaching and learning model. Institutionalized efforts to build on the momentum of MOOCs by stressing scalability, but potentially sacrificing critical forms of social learning in the process, raise a concern about the prospects of the MOOC movement, especially in light of the dominance of xMOOCs.

Problems of Implementation and Institutionalization

My research group analyzed pedagogical models employed in twenty-four MOOCs offered by an array of providers (Toven-Lindsey, Rhoads, and Berdan Lozano 2015). We purposely sampled these MOOCs on the basis of Anthony Biglan's (1973a, 1973b) model of academic disciplines, which built on Charles Percy Snow's (1959) classic book *The Two Cultures and the Scientific Revolution.* To be brief, Snow argued that disciplines may be classified as hard or soft based on the degree of stability of the basic theories undergirding them—hard fields

Table 1   MOOCs included in the study and purposely sampled based on
the Biglan model

	Hard	Soft
Pure Life	Biology Biology Biology	Philosophy Sociology Social Theory
Pure Non-Life	Statistics Statistics Physics	Geography English Composition Poetry
Applied Life	Medicine Nursing Public Health	Health & Climate Law Gaming
Applied Non-Life	Chemical Engineering Engineering Statistics Computer Graphics	Product Development Development Economics Macroeconomics

Source: From Toven-Lindsey, Rhoads, and Berdan Lozano (2015).

have more lasting theories, while in soft fields the theories often are revised (theories are on soft ground, so to speak). The Biglan model adds two additional dimensions: applied vs. pure and life vs. non-life. This results in an eightfold typology for grouping academic fields of study. In seeking to examine a range of MOOCs, we purposely selected courses across this eightfold typology of disciplines. The study also sought to maximize the range of instructional tools used so we might better understand the diversity of teaching methods employed in MOOCs; we specifically aimed to examine the degree to which forms of social learning are incorporated into MOOC teaching and learning designs. Table 1 reveals the list of courses we purposely sampled and where they fit within Biglan's framework. The courses were offered by the following providers: Canvas Network, Coursera, Education Portal, edX, Faculty Project/Udemy, MR University, NovoEd, MIT Open Course Ware Scholar, CMU Open Learning Initiative, Open Michigan, OpenLearning, Open Yale Courses, Saylor.org/Saylor University, Sofia Project, Udacity, and Webcast Berkeley.

Based on the "teaching approach framework" from J. B. Arbaugh and Raquel Benbunin-Fich (2006), we analyzed the courses in terms of the pedagogical strategies employed, based on two intersecting dimensions. The first is the epistemological dimension, which ranges from objectivist to constructivist views of knowledge. An objectivist position stresses the idea that knowledge and truth exist in the world to be discovered through inquiry; it assumes that a single objective reality exists and that knowledge should be transmitted from teacher to student. The constructivist approach emphasizes knowledge and truth as created or constructed through inquiry. Given that knowledge and truth do not simply exist, as if handed down by god or nature, constructivists recognize that multiple realities exist; hence, there is a provisional quality to knowing.

The second dimension to the teaching approach framework—the social dimension—focuses on whether teaching and learning approaches stress individual or group strategies for promoting student engagement and understanding. Building a typology based on the intersection of the two dimensions leads to four different ways of thinking about teaching and learning: objectivist-individual, objectivist-group, constructivist-individual, and constructivist-group. The latter form of teaching and learning—constructivist-group—reflects some of the basic principles undergirding connectivism and MOOCs in their idealized form.

Of the twenty-four MOOCs we analyzed, none utilized a constructivist-group approach as the dominant modality for engaging learners during the course. Roughly a third of the courses included a constructivist-group activity of some kind, including peer-reviewed writing assignments, group debates or discussions, and in a few instances, live video conferencing with an instructor, but these strategies tended to be short-lived and in no manner or form defined the dominant teaching and learning strategy. Indeed, the dominant modality for framing teaching and learning among the sampled MOOCs was the objectivist-individual approach. All of the sampled courses depended heavily on elements of the objectivist-individual approach, while instances of effective use of the constructivist-group approach were infrequent (Toven-Lindsey, Rhoads, and Berdan Lozano 2015). Discussion boards were available in the majority of courses, but they were mostly used by peers or teaching assistants to convey particular assignments or concepts as opposed to facilitating meaningful collaboration and group-oriented knowledge construction. Teachers in only a few of the MOOCs used the boards to supplement their instruction by posting discussion topics or incorporating group activities into the curriculum.

Findings from this study indicate that provider-driven MOOCs or xMOOCs face a challenge in developing and implementing rich social learning environments. Keeping in mind that the constructivist-group approach described in our study shares some basic principles with the connectivist learning model advanced by Siemens (2004, 2013), Alec Couros (2009), and others, the fact that it was such a marginal strategy in the MOOCs we studied is telling. These findings speak directly to the challenges of implementing meaningful teaching and learning strategies when economy-of-scale issues are so prevalent.

A key issue undermining the development and advance of the type of connectivist-oriented MOOCs originally envisioned by Siemens and Downes is that as the MOOC movement expanded in size and scope, it also was refashioned. Increasingly, higher education reform advocates, educational innovators, and entrepreneurs saw the credit-bearing and credentialing potential of MOOCs. Once MOOCs were conceptualized, developed, and then marketed as potential courses for credit or as part of a credential program, providers needed to develop ways of verifying student learning outcomes and validating the learner's experience. Thus, instead of the lifelong learning ideals that had given rise to the Siemens-Downes MOOC, with great connectivist opportunities for ongoing learner-directed course development, institutionalized and provider-driven MOOCs holding the potential for course credit and credentialing changed the nature of the game. For some, this led to the need to identify two different types of MOOCs: cMOOCs and xMOOCs, the latter representing the institutionalized version, often exhibiting compromised connectivist qualities.

What seemed initially like an awesome experiment in transformative democratic education in the age of the Internet instead shifted toward an innovative solution to address problems of higher education access. This is the idea that William Bowen (2013) raised in his book *Higher Education in the Digital Age*, when he asked: "Is it realistic to imagine that online learning is a 'fix' (at least in part) to the cost disease?" (2). By the "cost disease" (also known as the "Baumol effect") he was referencing out-of-control college costs over the past few decades, which he saw as partly tied to the labor-intensive quality of education.[3] In higher education, as Bowen argued, "There is less opportunity than in other sectors to increase productivity" (3), given that so much of the cost of the education industry is tied to labor. He described this same phenomenon in the arts, noting an example drawn from Robert Frank of Cornell University: "While productivity gains have made it possible to assemble cars with only a tiny fraction of the labor that was once required, it still takes four musicians nine minutes to perform Beethoven's String Quartet No. 4 in C minor, just as it did in the 19th century" (4).

Bowen focused mainly on the issue of productivity in higher education and the potential for online education to reduce the costs of inputs (e.g., faculty labor) as well as increasing outputs (e.g., student learning). He adopted a common definition of productivity as "the ratio of outputs to the inputs used to produce them" (6). So for Bowen, who at one time had strongly questioned the idea of using technology to enhance higher education productivity, there are two key ways that MOOCs and other forms of online education might impact productivity: "through determined efforts to reduce costs—that is, we need to focus more energy on lowering the denominator of the productivity ratio; and through new ways of increasing the student-learning component of the numerator of the ratio, principally by raising completion rates and lowering time-to-degree" (9). MOOCs hold the potential to impact both the denominator (labor costs) and the numerator (student degree completion). MOOCs may affect labor costs by producing courses that take advantage of reusable digitized materials and that are offered at a massive level, thus reducing the number of courses needing to be offered overall. MOOCs may decrease the time students need to complete degrees by offering greater flexibility for taking courses, especially for students at financially stressed colleges and universities where getting locked out of a course may be a common problem. Bowen was clear to note, though, that he did not see online education as a panacea for what he described as "deep-seated educational problems . . . rooted in social issues, fiscal dilemmas, and national priorities" (70). He instead stressed that online education might be part of a complex answer, although he warned that the "media frenzy associated with MOOCs" might lead some business-minded types "to embrace too tightly the MOOC approach" (70).

The productivity discourse tended to dominate discussion about MOOCs and their contribution to higher education. The original idea of the MOOC stressing connectivism was eventually refashioned to help address the pressing demands facing public colleges and universities in an age of declining financial support. The MOOC as a model for lifelong learning transformed into a cost-effective solution for serving the needs of low-income and working-class students attending financially strapped public institutions and perhaps some privates as well.

A few higher education analysts suspected early on that this was a problematic strategy, given that research evidence over the years had shown that the least educationally prepared students tend to need higher levels of face-to-face support and benefit significantly from peer support. Alexander Astin (1993,

1999), one of the leading U.S. scholars in the area of student learning, criticized MOOC advocates for ignoring past research that might have informed a deeper understanding of the role of online education. At a talk in Santa Barbara, presented as part of the thirteenth annual Conversation on the Liberal Arts and sponsored by the Gaede Institute for the Liberal Arts, where Siemens gave the opening address titled "What Will MOOCs Do to Traditional Education?," Astin (2014) highlighted how empirical research studies "repeatedly identified specific educational practices and experiences that tend to promote positive educational outcomes for students." Astin further argued that such findings tend to be ignored by the most ardent MOOC advocates. He specifically noted the positive impact of the following educational strategies:

- Frequent student-faculty interaction
- Frequent student-student interaction
- Generous expenditures on student services
- Frequent interracial interaction
- Frequent use of interdisciplinary courses
- Frequent use of courses that emphasize writing
- Frequent use of narrative evaluations
- Infrequent use of multiple choice exams
- Involvement of students in independent research
- Involvement of students in faculty research
- Participation in service learning courses
- Participation in study abroad programs
- Involvement in co-curricular activities

Astin went on to conclude that the typical MOOC "makes it very difficult for the student to be exposed to any of these practices. . . . And even if the MOOC student manages to conduct independent research, who is going to mentor that student during the process and who is going to review the finished product?"

Several of Astin's concerns are addressed in a few of the most advanced MOOCs; some include writing assignments and offer elaborate mechanisms for peer feedback on papers. But again, when MOOCs are scaled up with the goal of reaching thousands of users, they are often forced to drop or compromise the social learning components, given the need to maximize efficiency while minimizing costs. Under such conditions, the richness of the learning experience, especially as it relates to contact with a faculty instructor, is minimized. Herein is the crux of the problem: What appears to be an innovative model for lifelong learning (cMOOCs), a transformative democratic form of education that perhaps is most beneficial to professional communities of practice, becomes something entirely different when used as a substitute for meaningful face-to-face courses for traditional college-going populations (xMOOCs). This seems especially problematic when xMOOCs are offered as replacement courses targeting the most disadvantaged learners, such as low-income and working-class students at financially strapped public colleges and universities. Many such students come from under-resourced K-12 schools and need greater, not lesser, support during the college years. If xMOOCs are to be used in such a manner, then additional support must be offered to enhance student success.

xMOOCs and Grounds for Optimism

Problems associated with xMOOCs are partially evident by the high attrition rates and low performance of students in MOOCs, especially those used as substitutes for developmental or remedial courses, as was the case with San Jose State University's experiment with Udacity. For MOOCs to be truly transformative, they cannot simply be thrust on students at underfunded public institutions without additional teaching and learning support or incentivization. What might MOOCs look like when they take such concerns seriously? Possible answers to this question come from the MOOC Research Initiative (MRI) funded by the Gates Foundation.

One MRI study in particular offers optimism about the potential of MOOCs to better prepare students for college-level work. A study led by Mark Warschauer (2014) and conducted at UC Irvine revealed that at-risk learners may benefit from MOOCs as preparation for university-level STEM work when the motivation is significant. In the case of this study, the source of motivation was this: If pre-college students who failed to achieve a qualifying SAT score of 550 or higher completed a biology preparation course (Bio Prep MOOC) with distinction, then they could transfer into the biology major at UCI after one quarter instead of three quarters, bypassing the prerequisites typically required of students with lower SAT math scores. In the end, the students scoring below 550 performed at a level comparable to those with higher SAT math scores (maybe even a little better), although the latter group did not have a similar source of motivation (they were already able to enroll in the major). A key aspect of this study is that although Bio Prep MOOC was open to an unlimited number of enrollees, a subpopulation—those students admitted to UCI and hoping to major in biology—were incentivized by the chance to enroll in the major earlier than is normally the case. Interestingly, 68 percent of "weak math" UCI students completed the course compared to 62 percent of "strong math" students (only 9% of the overall enrollees completed the course). Perhaps more compelling, a greater percentage of "weak math" than "strong math" students earned a distinction certificate (37% to 23%). Two issues are key here. First, the study did not focus on the entire Bio Prep MOOC enrollment population but on a subpopulation of students already admitted to UCI. Second, a sizeable portion of the UCI students (the "weak math" students) was further incentivized by the chance to enroll early in biology. The strategy of engaging a subpopulation of MOOC takers and then incentivizing them in some manner seems promising. But it is also necessary to keep in mind that Bio Prep MOOC was not a substitute for a required face-to-face course but was additional preparation for college students.

Other preliminary MRI findings coming out in 2014 revealed promise as well, but unfortunately methodological shortcomings of some of the studies left more questions than answers. For example, a study of the University of Wisconsin System College Readiness Math MOOC reported gains in math ability for students completing the course. A problem, though, is that the pre-test and post-test instruments were identical, based on basic algebra questions. It seems logical to expect that any math exam repeated after a brief time span is likely to result in a higher score, especially in light of an instructional intervention subsequent the first testing (the UW math MOOC involved nine mathematics modules with quizzes after each). On a positive note, the study reported that 81 percent of students completing the post-test instrument indicated improved confidence in their math skills. Again, as was the case with UC Irvine's Bio Prep MOOC, the UW math MOOC was designed as an extra preparatory course equivalent to remedial or developmental course work. Both MOOCs were additive and in this sense offered no cost savings. The presumed benefits of course are associated with having better prepared students.

Overall, the MRI studies offer a somewhat contradictory array of findings, with some pointing to the innovative potential of MOOCs and others highlighting a general lack of active engagement, limited transfer of learning to practice, and low completion rates.[4] Clearly though, there are important teaching and learning issues to consider in adopting xMOOCs as a strategy for expanding higher education access. For example, the motivation of MOOC participants appears to be a major factor in predicting student persistence, as two additional MRI studies reported (Poellhuber, Roy, Bouchoucha, and Anderson 2014; Wang and Baker 2014). Of course, many observers assumed as much, given the wide range of reasons participants might have for participating in a MOOC. I say more about these and other pedagogical concerns in chapter 4.

Concluding Thoughts

A key distinction is made throughout this book between cMOOCs, primarily oriented toward self-directed learners and based on connectivist teaching and learning theory, and xMOOCs, the more institutionalized version of the MOOC and the one more likely to be envisioned as addressing problems of college access. Although cMOOCs seem well suited for adult learners and professional communities of practice, the challenges of implementing complex methodologies associated with connectivist teaching and learning make this version of the MOOC difficult to translate to traditional college-going populations and the goals of scalability. However, facets of social learning linked to connectivism and cMOOCs should be considered when developing xMOOCs, given the potential benefits of engaging online learners in group-oriented learning experiences. Additionally, although xMOOCs hold potential for reducing course production costs and supporting student degree attainment, their shortcomings must be considered if they truly are to contribute to expanding college access. In particular, xMOOCs need to develop additional mechanisms for supporting traditional college students and especially educationally disadvantaged students. In the following chapter I delve into this concern more deeply, while also delineating several key problems that pose challenges to the MOOC movement overall.

4

Blowback and Resistance to the MOOC Movement

The goal of this chapter is to make sense of some of the MOOC criticism arising primarily from 2013 to 2014. In part, my intent in delving more thoroughly into the critique of MOOCs is to develop a deeper understanding of the movement's potential; such a critique necessarily must acknowledge basic practical, conceptual, and ideological limitations of MOOCs as a form of educational innovation. Accordingly, I focus on five key problems that point to obstacles to the success of MOOCs and the overall movement: (1) the problem of epistemology, (2) the problem of pedagogy, (3) the problem of hegemony, (4) the problem of diversity, and (5) the problem of faculty labor.[1] These problems to varying degrees help explain why the much-heralded revolution in higher education seemingly had stalled by 2014.

As I note in chapter 1, the *New York Times* declared 2012 the Year of the MOOC. Less than two years later, though, the *Chronicle of Higher Education* asked if 2014 would become "The Year the Media Stopped Caring about MOOCs" (Kolowich 2014e). Ignoring the obvious irony that the *Chronicle* itself was partially responsible for MOOC Madness (Rhoads 2013) in the first place—the "media frenzy," as William Bowen (2013, 70) described it—and that apparently by early 2014 its editorial staff had decided to back off on its coverage, what had changed? Was higher education simply in the middle of its own "Jetpack Moment," with a variety of networking and computing technologies maturing around the same time, as Jeffrey Young (2013) argued in *Beyond the MOOC Hype?* Did we witness a perfect storm of sorts, technologically speaking? Certainly by early 2014 the storm had calmed, if not passed. This was obvious by the lack of enthusiasm for MOOCs among many students, professors, administrators, and policy makers; even some of the biggest MOOC advocates had backtracked.

A dampening of MOOC enthusiasm is further revealed by results of the annual Campus Computing Survey of information technology administrators: Although 2013 results indicated widespread support for MOOCs as "a viable model for the effective delivery of online education," the 2014 version reported lukewarm support, with only 38 percent of respondents seeing MOOCs as viable. Only 19 percent saw MOOCs as capable of generating revenue, down from the previous year's 29 percent (Koenig 2014). So what had become of the revolution that Daphne Koller and Sebastian Thrun had so braggadociously ushered in?

The fact that a shift in attitude toward MOOCs had taken place was evidenced by the remarks given by new University of California president Janet Napolitano during an interview with Mark Baldassare, president of the Public Policy Institute of California. Napolitano responded to one of Baldassare's questions about how online education fit within her initiatives:

> I think there's a developing consensus that online learning is a tool for the tool box, where higher education is concerned; that it is not a silver bullet the way it was originally portrayed to be. It's a lot harder than it looks. And, by the way, if you do it right, it doesn't save all that much money, because you still have to have an opportunity for students to interact with either a teaching assistant or an assistant professor or professor at some level. And preparing the courses, if they're really going to be top-quality, is an investment as well. (Kolowich 2014d)

The article went on to contrast Napolitano's remarks with those of California's governor, Jerry Brown, who had pushed for a "pilot partnership" with Udacity, which of course stumbled significantly. Arguably, problems associated with the Udacity project played a significant role in stemming the tide of unchecked MOOC optimism.

At the heart of Udacity's failures in California are basic problems that most online education platforms face. These problems primarily concern the epistemological and pedagogical limitations of the xMOOC model in particular and of online education more generally. Briefly, these limitations pertain to shortcomings in how knowledge is conceived and how relationships between teachers and students are structured. The realities of such problems are unlikely to be acknowledged by the most ardent supporters of the high-tech education revolution. There are, however, potential solutions to these problems, and I offer examples drawn from cMOOCs and some of the more creative xMOOCs.

Issues beyond the epistemological and pedagogical also arose throughout 2013. The growing dominance of a few university-based providers—namely, Harvard, MIT, and Stanford—raised red flags for many faculty and administrators committed to an institutionally diverse higher education system. Questions arose about whether public university students should be expected to get their lectures from online professors operating out of elite private universities. Scholars working in the international realm questioned the undampened enthusiasm of MOOC advocates, with many of the latter suggesting that courses developed at Western universities could somehow solve the woes of higher education in developing regions of the world, such as in parts of Africa. Still other critiques raised concerns about how MOOC advocates, as well as OCW proponents, tended to see online learners simply as entities situated behind a computer screen—as opposed to viewing them as having unique characteristics linked to race, gender, sexuality, and physical ability, among other identities. How could the critically important questions about diversity in higher education that had been raised over the past thirty years be so absent from discussions of the MOOC and OCW movements? Finally, concerns emerged about the implications MOOCs had for faculty labor. Critics wondered how the overall system of higher education was likely to benefit from more and more university courses being taught by a handful of star professors, almost always from elite private universities, who would now provide the academic labor for a new type of easily reproduced course—the xMOOC. What was to become of faculty no longer needed to develop course materials and offer lectures? For whom was this beneficial? These sorts of questions frame the thrust of the discussion in this chapter.[2]

The Problem of Epistemology

One of the most basic challenges confronting the MOOC movement concerns limitations in the nature of knowledge suitable for delivery through online mechanisms when economy-of-scale issues are prioritized. Although connectivist versions of teaching and learning advanced through cMOOCs lend themselves to a complex view of knowledge, the same cannot be said for the vast majority of MOOCs, typically offered in the form of xMOOCs. In the years following the first MOOCs, three issues surfaced to pose a challenge to connectivist teaching and learning modalities: (1) efforts to reach more traditional college age students (roughly 18–23 years old), (2) efforts to increase the scalability of the university course, and (3) efforts to connect MOOCs to credentialing. All three of these efforts were linked to broad concerns about expanding college access in light of both growing consumer demand and reductions in public funding. As a result, the majority of MOOCs developed in this context tended to move away from the connectivist strategies of the earliest MOOCs and instead reflected teaching and learning practices consistent with a mass approach to course development and assessment. With heavy emphasis on the *massive* aspect of the MOOC, course materials and content delivery strategies were consistent with a foundationalist epistemology; that is, many xMOOCs reflected a more static view of knowledge as akin in many ways to facts and information. This amounted to a significant epistemological shift by comparison to what early MOOC advocates had envisioned.

The first MOOC developed and implemented by George Siemens and Stephen Downes was an innovative experiment in promoting networked learning within the context of a community of practice—the community being adult and lifelong learning professionals. In the realm of experimental design, Siemens and Downes could hardly have selected a better set of subjects for their original MOOC, given the educational level of the course's participants, not to mention the emphasis of the field on self-directed learning. But eighteen- and nineteen-year olds struggling with basic mathematics or sociological principles are different from adult education professionals. Thus, when MOOCs increasingly were designed and targeted for traditional-age college students, especially those needing remedial interventions, problems became apparent. The reality that MOOCs seemed less of a revolutionary strategy for educating hordes of undergraduates contributed to the cooling off of the MOOC movement during 2013.

When a shift is made from cMOOCs geared toward professional communities of practice to xMOOCs targeting large numbers of undergraduates in lower-level or remedial courses, the nature of course content and delivery is likely to undergo a transformation. For example, as MOOC course designers and providers began to target lower-level undergraduate course work, they had to take into account the technological skill level of course takers; although most traditional-age undergraduates were weaned on the Internet and telecommunication devices, this does not mean they are as tech-savvy as adult educators knowledgeable of the world of online learning. It's one thing to text friends all day and communicate through Facebook and Twitter, but it's quite another to use Internet-based technologies to research complex topics and ideas. Additionally, developing economy-of-scale courses necessitated certain adjustments, such as discarding more advanced forms of networked social learning or eliminating any real opportunity to interact directly with an instructor. Scaling up to a massive level also involved compromises in terms of having an instructor available to evaluate student performance. The latter became an important issue when MOOCs were fashioned as courses for credit or leading to a credential in the form of a badge, certificate, or degree.

A variety of forces then helped to push xMOOC design and development toward a less complex view of knowledge, one that could easily take advantage of, for example, computerized grading and assessment. Whether conducted by the course provider or a testing center such as Pearson VUE, computerized scoring was practically a necessity for MOOCs motivated by economy-of-scale issues.

My criticism of xMOOCs and their tendency to rely on more simplistic conceptions of knowledge is not intended as a blanket statement. There have been and continue to be excellent examples of how xMOOC design might incorporate sophisticated mechanisms for student feedback and assessment in a manner consistent with constructivist teaching and learning ideals. Coursera has worked hard to incorporate Community TAs (volunteer teaching assistants) in its courses, potentially offering more dialogical forms of course feedback. Also, research from the MOOC Research Initiative (MRI) has shown that xMOOCs under certain conditions can use peer-to-peer writing as a strategy to generate important learning conversations among MOOC takers, a finding true for both an English and a chemistry MOOC (Comer and Canelas 2014). The problem, though, is that constructivist xMOOCs tend to be the exception and not the rule.

The success of the early cMOOCs was in part based on the fact that the professional adult educators enrolled were well equipped for developing their own learning communities and working out elaborative online mechanisms for communication and networked learning. They taught themselves in many ways, just as the course designers had hoped they would. Other online learners who enroll in MOOCs also may possess advanced understandings of Internet-based applications and creative strategies for promoting collective intelligence. But for many traditional-aged college students, staff or instructional support is necessary for building the technical competence and content knowledge required to succeed in online courses. Also, the goal for student learning becomes less about group accomplishment (as in promoting collective intelligence) and instead is more oriented toward an individual's performance (as in individual intelligence); this too serves to isolate the individual learner and further necessitates instructional support. In order to be successful then, xMOOCs targeting traditional-aged college students need to offer a minimal level of support. But how does this occur in an environment prioritizing scalability, where limiting course-related costs is a necessity? Here, I stress that xMOOCs largely have been seen as a cost-savings measure, in line with issues of productivity and the higher education "cost disease" raised in William Bowen (2013), especially for cash-strapped public universities.

The possibility of reaching hundreds of students through one course initially was what caught the attention of many MOOC supporters. But when MOOCs target hundreds or even thousands of learners, certain adjustments are necessary. For example, instead of employing a wide range of creative connectivist-oriented learning opportunities, a MOOC offering potential course credit to hordes of learners is much more likely to simply involve the most basic online education modalities: reading lists, recorded lectures, lecture notes or PowerPoint slides, some quizzes or exams to take online, and so forth. There may be chat rooms or discussion boards through which students converse or post comments. However, the more advanced ideals of connectivist learning involving digital platforms and complex and time-consuming forms of social learning, utilized to promote group projects and collective intelligence, are often nonexistent. When teaching and learning processes instead are tied to a more foundationalist view of knowledge, where there are few if any opportunities for students to engage in meaningful forms of social learning and dialogue, they become a disempowering form of education lacking opportunities for analyzing the connections between knowledge and power.

Knowledge, Power, and MOOCs

One of the most serious concerns I have about the reduction of knowledge to information in the teaching and learning environment of the MOOC, most specifically the xMOOC, is the limited opportunity to examine and critique the role of power relative to knowledge claims. The work of Michel Foucault (1972, 1979, 1980) is particularly helpful in terms of understanding the relationship between power and knowledge, including the idea that power exists in all social arenas and frames the types of discourses that become central or peripheral to various fields or disciplines. For Foucault, power does not simply operate to deny or punish; it also serves a positive function, establishing the very norms by which ideas, actions, and identities are judged. Indeed, Foucault saw power operating through "a net-like organization" (1980, 98) and existing like a "web of power" (116), evident to some extent in all social relations and always having the potential to normalize behavior. Obviously, in selecting terms and phrases like "net-like" and "web of power" he was not referencing the World Wide Web; he was writing mostly in the 1960s and 1970s, and though arguably a brilliant thinker, he was not Nostradamus. Nonetheless, the imagery is apt: what's more "net-like" than the Internet and a scaled-up xMOOC reaching thousands of online learners?

Foucault saw power operating as a productive force in that it served to produce behaviors and understandings, as opposed to simply denying or repressing them. He saw schools, prisons, and hospitals, for example, as key institutions having productive capacities to define normative behaviors and identities, in terms of the student, the citizen/criminal, and the mentally ill. Foucault elaborated his thinking most clearly in his classic work *Discipline and Punish*, wherein he likened the totality of the forces of productive power to the forms of surveillance captured by Jeremy Bentham's ideal of the Panopticon—a circular prison structure with a central tower where all the actions of the prisoners are observable by a guard. The Panopticon serves as a metaphor for the ways that modern society produces norms of behavior and truth through the positive operations of power. A more concrete example of Foucault's thinking comes from his book *The History of Sexuality* (1978), in which he highlights how the dominant historical discourse surrounding sexuality produced a norming effect. Countering arguments that discussions of sexuality were suppressed, Foucault pointed out how the discourse of sexuality was pervasive, although typically framed in a manner that normalized heterosexual relations. MOOCs structured as vehicles for advancing facts and information to online learners as a form of discourse have the potential to offer one more mechanism for elevating a particular version of knowledge (and reality) in a manner consistent with Foucault's notion of power's productive capacity.

Given the limitations of scalable MOOCs—again, I'm not talking about cMOOCs—course-related knowledge is more likely than not to be framed as information with little opportunity for critique or deconstruction. Power becomes invisible, and yet it operates aggressively, asserting a normative vision of the basic topic, subject, or field. To borrow from another French theorist, Jean-François Lyotard, "Who decides the conditions of truth?" (1984, 7). In the context of the typical xMOOC, the instructor or course developer decides the conditions of truth. And more times than not, the course developer is a faculty member at an elite university such as Harvard, MIT, Yale, or Stanford—institutions not known for their diverse ways of understanding and conceptualizing knowledge.

Let us consider some examples to highlight my point. Take for example literature offerings by Open Yale Courses (OYC) organized by the university's Department of English. In the spring of 2014 the offerings included "Introduction to Theory of Literature" with Paul Fry, "Milton" with John Rogers, "Modern Poetry" with Langdon Hammer, and "The American Novel since 1945" with Amy Hungerford. The course website informs us that Hungerford is a highly regarded professor of English specializing in twentieth- and twenty-first-century American literature and a founder of the Post-45 movement. As of 2009, she had authored two books, at least according to the website: The Holocaust of Texts: Genocide, Literature, and Personification as well as Postmodern Belief: American Literature and Religion Since 1960. The reading list for the course looks particularly exciting to me, with readings from some of my favorite authors such as Richard Wright, Vladimir Nabokov, Jack Kerouac, J. D. Salinger, and Toni Morrison, among others. Anyone can participate in the online version of the course, simply by keeping up with the readings and observing the recorded lectures. The online offering parallels the actual for-credit course taken by Yale students, taught and recorded in 2008. "The American Novel since 1945" is a good example of commonly structured OCW material, easily converted to a MOOC simply by adding elements of synchronicity and assessment. The OYC version includes no writing assignment, as there is no real instructor to read any materials from online learners. Of course, online users are free to form their own networked spaces for sharing work and conversing, although OYC does not offer any assistance in forming networked spaces. The website notes that video and audio files also are available at YouTube and iTunes.

At least two issues arise here relative to my discussion of epistemology and the role of power. First, a complex area of scholarship—the American novel—is pretty much reduced to Amy Hungerford's version of it. Her interpretation gets positioned as the normalized analysis of the American novel. This is not a criticism of her but of the limitations of the structure of this manner of course offering. There is no opportunity for online learners to question or to criticize the course content, except through the online communities and networks they construct themselves. However, this is unlikely to occur in light of the lack of support from OYC. Further, OYC does not provide any clear guidance on how online learners might interact with the instructor, and given the possibility of countless learners engaging the material, it is hard to imagine Hungerford actually having the time to respond to those who might track her down through e-mail; as a professor at Yale University, she presumably is heavily engaged in research and must limit her interactions with online learners.

A second issue arises in light of credentialing and the need for student assessment. OYC does not offer the opportunity for course credit except for those Yale students enrolled in the course in 2008. The OYC website makes this clear: "Open Yale Courses does not grant degrees or certificates. Nor does it offer direct access to Yale faculty. Open Yale Courses aims to expand access to educational materials of a selection of Yale courses for those who wish to learn. Its purpose is not to duplicate a Yale education." This statement aligns with the terms of the early OCW/MOOC ideal of democratizing course materials and learning opportunities. However, for politicians, policy makers, and institutional leaders seeking to further higher education access by taking advantage of the OCW/MOOC movements, this presents a problem. Hypothetically speaking, if an agency or other legitimizing entity (e.g., University of the People) were to step in and offer course credit, the entity would need to verify student learning in some manner or form; indeed, through a partnership with Coursera, Yale offers several such courses. But given the massiveness of xMOOCs, assuming some level of success, verification of learning outcomes most likely would be accomplished through a computer-scored multiple-choice exam. Herein lies part of the problem—such a solution further reinforces foundationalist elements of the course and reproduces forms of understanding counter to the critique of knowledge and power advanced by the likes of Foucault.

Face-to-face literature courses such as "The American Novel since 1945" typically involve analytical writing requirements in the form of a serious term paper. Such writing encourages students to develop their own ideas in a constructivist manner. Can MOOCs also include more constructivist forms of student learning and assessment, such as in asking students to develop and submit research papers? For example, why can't another entity beyond OYC build on Hungerford's course, or another offering such as "Modern Poetry" with Langdon Hammer, by adding writing requirements to be assessed by an instructor? After all, OYC seems to encourage the refashioning of the course based on statements at the website supporting "reusers," directing them to Yale's Creative Commons license and the "Terms of Use." The problem then becomes, how does a course provider offer instructional support for a massively open literature-based course? How many papers can one instructor read and grade, and here's the real catch—for free? "Massive" implies many online learners (potentially thousands), and "open" typically means free (and shareable as well). Of course, a legitimizing entity could reasonably charge to verify student learning outcomes for credit, but a legitimizer is unlikely to do so by asking online learners to submit writing samples, given economy-of-scale issues. That's just not profitable, keeping in mind some of the points Bowen (2013) raised about MOOCs and productivity. A few of the most diehard MOOC advocates have suggested the use of computer software to evaluate submitted research papers, but there are problems with such software, including the ability of writers to "game" the process (Perelman 2014). The MOOCs-for-credit idea poses difficult problems that ultimately undermine the revolutionary potential of the movement.

Stephen Downes (2013), writing at his blog *Half an Hour*, attempted to address the problem of assessment in a humanities MOOC in which a writing assignment might be expected of students. He responded to the following concern voiced by an instructor:

> I was wondering how they [MOOCs] might work with the humanities, as I teach Seventeenth-Century Literature, Shakespeare and other related subjects, which require research papers and final examinations. I can see using MOOCs for people who simply have a (non-credit) interest in these subjects, but I can't see myself marking 5,000 term papers, and a similar number of exams. Multiple-choice evaluation, as in science, is easily taken care of electronically, but not in the humanities. I am sure this looks like a naive question, but I think MOOCs are a wonderful idea for people who simply wish to enrich their knowledge.

Downes replied by offering several possible solutions including automated essay assessment and peer assessment. But both of these techniques are fraught with problems. As I note above, automated assessments can be gamed, not to mention the fact that their rigidity may undermine the creative facet of good writing. Peer assessments have problems as well (Piech et al. 2013), especially in terms of online learners lacking incentive and accountability to offer comments beyond the minimal, if they provide feedback at all (Rees 2013). No doubt recognizing some of these problems, Downes also suggested that an instructor could "bypass grading entirely," but this of course becomes a problem for learners hoping to obtain course credit.

Now one might easily argue that the epistemological limitations of a for-credit MOOC are not so different from those of the traditional lecture, especially those taking place in auditorium-like lecture halls. Surely in such settings students may disappear behind a newspaper, laptop, or iPhone. This hardly seems like an engaging form of teaching and learning in which students are apt to challenge the forms of knowledge and truth put forth by the instructor. On this point I partially agree, but why then reproduce forms of education that ought to be challenged in the first place? This is especially problematic in light of the tendency for the most vocal online education advocates to describe MOOCs as a revolutionary force aimed at transforming higher learning. If MOOCs reproduce a pedagogical model that has serious shortcomings, then how can they be revolutionary? Furthermore, even in a large lecture hall there is at least the potential for students to raise challenging questions from time to time, with the likelihood of an instructor's response. Or perhaps a conversation with classmates might arise subsequent to the lecture. This is not necessarily the case in the scaled-up xMOOC, where interactions with a real professor are rare and conversations with classmates are limited by a lack of face-to-face connection. Yes, there are advantages as well to the xMOOC, such as having thousands of potential classmates. And early MRI research findings tend to show the xMOOCs as preparatory or developmental courses offered to incoming college students may be quite helpful. But such courses were additive—they were not substitutes for face-to-face learning opportunities. Nothing presumably is lost when incoming college students are asked to complete a summer course—an xMOOC—in advance of their enrollment. This makes perfect sense if xMOOCs help incoming students develop knowledge, skills, or self-confidence prior to their first semester of coursework. But to replace some of those first-semester face-to-face courses with xMOOCs is a different matter altogether. So, it's not simply that the xMOOC model is problematic. Instead, a key issue relates to how they are to be used as educational tools.

The Problem of Pedagogy

What I call the problem of pedagogy is closely related to the problem of epistemology. I see problems relating to teaching strategies in xMOOCs as critical to understanding the present-day limitations of the overall MOOC movement. Whereas the problem of epistemology concerns the reality that knowledge is often reduced to information, to facts, and then conveyed to online learners who may need to demonstrate their mastery in pursuit of credentials, the problem of pedagogy focuses on the delivery mechanisms for conveying knowledge. In the context of xMOOCs, these mechanisms are generally one-directional. One-directional forms of teaching are not well suited for promoting the kind of critical thinking that allows learners to grapple with issues of power and domination relative to their experiences in the world (Freire 1970; Giroux 1988, 1990).

Despite their connectivist potential, in a world dominated by economy-of-scale issues, the typical MOOC is forced to rely on systems of content delivery reflective of what Paulo Freire (1970) described as the banking concept of education. Freire argued that dominant forms of education and teaching tend to conceptualize the teacher as the authority on knowledge, while students are seen as empty vessels to be filled with facts and information (here one gets the sense of how a particular view of knowledge—epistemology—is linked to pedagogy). He saw such forms of teaching as dehumanizing in that they tend to discourage the basic characteristics needed in fostering vibrant social lives, including curiosity and creativity. The standard view of teaching, according to Freire's critique, suggests that teachers more or less make a "bank deposit" of facts and information to the students' minds, which remain mostly passive. As Freire explained, "The teacher teaches and the students are taught; the teacher knows everything and the students know nothing; the teacher thinks and the students are thought about; the teacher talks and the students listen—meekly; the teacher disciplines and the students are disciplined" (59). Banking education is unidirectional, with information flowing from teacher to student. For some, it is hard to consider such teaching as involving knowledge, as real knowledge is far more likely to demand deeper dialogues and questioning on the part of students.

The counter to the banking model is what bell hooks (1994) described as engaged pedagogy, or liberatory pedagogy from Freire's perspective (this version of teaching is also described as critical pedagogy and sometimes as critical humanist education). Engaged pedagogy calls for teachers to play active roles in the educational process by facilitating dialogues and supporting students through their trials and tribulations as active participants in the construction of knowledge. Freire's goal is for students to develop a critical consciousness of the world around them and understand the ways that social forces have acted and continue to act upon their lives. The goal is not simply literacy but critical cultural literacy.

The typical delivery structure of xMOOCs does not encourage the development of the kind of critical consciousness Freire advocated. xMOOCs commonly include reading lists or articles posted online for students to read. Recorded lectures frequently are posted on a common site to be viewed by course takers, often at their own pace. PowerPoint slides and lecture notes may be made available for students to peruse. Students may be asked to post their reactions on a discussion board to be shared with other course participants, possibly generating reactions and counterpoints. Or, they may be divided into subgroups and asked to participate in focused discussions taking place in chat rooms, through virtual interaction apps, or at social media sites. The latter strategies begin to move away from the notion of banking education, but participation in discussion boards, social media, or online chat rooms can be an exasperating experience with course enrollees offering countless comments, some of which may seem off-topic or unconstructive, discouraging further participation by course takers. Given the challenges of constructing meaningful social learning experiences in large-scale MOOCs, beleaguered instructors often are left with few options but to fall back on one-directional forms of teaching.

Research evidence on MOOCs tends to support the argument that the teaching and learning environment is less than ideal for active learner participation. For example, research findings coming out of the University of Pennsylvania's Alliance for Higher Education and Democracy (AHEAD) revealed that MOOCs have very few active learners and that engagement in courses falls off dramatically after about two weeks. Their research paper, "The Life Cycle of a Million MOOC Users," by Laura Perna, director of AHEAD, and co-authors (2013), was presented at the MOOC Research Initiative's December 2013 conference at the University of Texas. The Perna group analyzed a million MOOC users participating in sixteen Penn courses offered through Coursera from June 2012 to June 2013. They found that MOOC usage, in every category studied—from the number of course participants, to the number accessing course websites, to lectures observed, to quizzes submitted—dropped off dramatically throughout the duration of the MOOCs studied.[3] Of course, the huge enrollments of the Penn MOOCs also highlight their success in terms of generating interest among a diverse array of MOOC users, many of whom simply sought to satisfy their curiosity. xMOOCs assessed in this manner are no doubt hugely successful.

The student-engagement findings of Perna's group are similar to those reported by researchers at Glasgow Caledonian University and Harvard University. The latter study was conducted by Colin Milligan and Allison Littlejohn of the Caledonian Academy (a research center focused on technology-enhanced professional learning) and Obiageli Ukadike of the Harvard Medical School. They studied the experiences of learners taking "The Fundamentals of Clinical Trials," a MOOC offered by Harvard Medical School through the edX platform and intended for health professionals, by surveying some four hundred course participants and interviewing a subsample. The course was selected on the basis that it utilized many of the standard teaching methods of MOOCs, including video lectures, discussion boards, and online exams. Key findings pointed to the course encouraging passive learning and failing to utilize the knowledge and expertise brought to the course by a diverse group of health care professionals. As Littlejohn noted at her website, "Little by Littlejohn":

> Learners focused on activities such as watching videos and taking tests, with little evidence of learners relating new knowledge into practice, or of connecting to their peers though the discussion board. To be effective, professional learning should provide opportunities to integrate theoretical and practical knowledge. But even those learners who said they wanted to improve their professional practice did not integrate the scientific knowledge they learned through the MOOC with practical, on-the-job learning.[4]

Littlejohn's points reinforce the central argument here that xMOOCs struggle to engage students in active forms of learning.[5] A few exceptions to this pattern of inactive learning and disengagement exist, such as MRI findings reported by John Whitmer (2014) relative to student success in a "Basic Skills English" writing MOOC. Nonetheless, with passive learning so common in the xMOOC learning environment, what chance do learners have of developing the kinds of critical literacy skills consistent with a Freirian perspective? Of course, one could make the same charges against large face-to-face lectures, but again, do we really want to reproduce the shortcomings of the modern university in the name of high-tech innovation?

MOOCs and Critical Literacy

The critique to this point tends to reflect the xMOOC variety. But what do we know about the more advanced cMOOCs? Are they also vulnerable to the critique of pedagogy suggested here? Rita Kop (2011) conducted an analysis of connectivist learning and its shortcomings. She studied two cMOOCs— "Critical Literacies" (CritLit, with 377 participants) and "Personal Learning

Environments, Networks, and Knowledge" (PLENK, with 1,610 participants)—in conjunction with the National Research Council of Canada's Institute for Information Technology. She highlighted the need for promoting more critical views of online content, noting that one of the challenges to connectivist learning includes the need for critical literacies, which she tended to see as the ability to understand and critique power relations in Internet-based networks. She argued that part of the solution involves social interaction. In other words, students interacting in the context of online learning communities may contribute to the development of critical literacies through their exchange of ideas, including raising critical questions about the links between power and knowledge. As she explained, online learners must have the ability to "not only use network resources, but also to look at them critically" for the purpose of appropriating and redesigning them.

A key part of developing critical literacy for meaningful online learning is a recognition that the Internet and the web of knowledge and information available is not the democratic space so many claim it to be. Kop (2011) made this point as well, arguing "that power relations prevent network 'surfers' from having access to all information at the same level" (23). As she noted, this is further supported by Albert-Laszlo Barabasi's work involving a web-mapping project. As Barabasi explained, "The most intriguing result of our Web-mapping project was the *complete* absence of democracy, fairness, and egalitarian values on the Web. We learned that the topology of the Web prevents us from seeing anything but a mere handful of the billion documents out there" (2003, 56).

Kop went on to argue that in order to develop critical literacies, online learners "need to have a certain level of creativity and innovative thinking, in addition to a competency in using ICT [information and communications technology] applications. . . . Learners need to be flexible to be able to adapt to new situations and are also expected to solve problems that they come across during their learning journey in this complex learning environment" (23). Can we expect traditional-aged students, especially many of the students at our public universities coming from under-resourced K-12 schools, to have these kinds of skill sets early in their college careers? Certainly some will have the necessary conceptual and practical skills, but a large body of work on social class, cultural capital, and habitus, mostly building on the theoretical work of Pierre Bourdieu, suggests otherwise for the majority (MacLeod 1995; Maldonado, Rhoads, and Buenavista 2005; McDonough 1997). Here one must also consider the digital divide and the role social class plays in reinforcing inequalities linked to access and use of technology (Kapitzke 2000; Norris 2001). Clearly, there is a key role for teachers and faculty members to play in supporting students' growth, both in terms of technological proficiency and also with regard to critically examining content they access online.

When we consider the ways in which various forms of power may actually shape web-based content, the theoretical contributions of Foucault (in terms of power operating in a net-like manner practically everywhere) and Freire are unified: Freirian objectives to promote critical consciousness encourage analyzing the basic structures of power undergirding the Internet and the many sources of knowledge and information proliferating in such an environment. Although connectivist forms of teaching and learning represent an advance in terms of promoting the kind of social learning necessary in an increasingly networked world, they fail to adequately critique their own democratic claims.

The lack of critical analysis of MOOCs and Internet-based courses is most obvious among some of the biggest OCW advocates, who often speak of the movement and the role of Internet-based information and technologies as "flattening the world" in a manner expressed by Thomas Friedman (2005). A good example of what I see as the uncritical optimism associated with online education and the Internet comes from Curtis Bonk's *The World is Open*. Bonk argued that the world automatically progresses as more information and courses are included on the Internet: "Web technology offers new hope for educating the citizens of this planet. It is the opening up of education that ultimately makes a flatter or more robust economic world possible. In the twenty-first century, education trumps economy as the key card to participation in the world" (2009, 7–8). Bonk went on to add that as a consequence of greater access to Internet-based information, "The reins of power have indeed shifted," given that most everyone working in education is now "learner-centered" (39). This is a provocative take on the state of affairs in education, given that Bonk's point flies in the face of numerous claims that educational institutions, particularly college and universities, operate more like economic enterprises than ever before with students increasingly defined as consumers (Aronowitz 2000; Bok 2003; Giroux 2002; Rhoads and Szelényi 2011; Slaughter and Rhoades 2004). In terms of the "reins of power" shifting, the growing gap between the wealthiest and the poorest in the United States and around the world, as highlighted most obviously by the driving passion of the Occupy Wall Street movement, tends to suggest otherwise. Clearly, there is much need for a more critical discourse to be incorporated not only into pedagogical models undergirding MOOCs but also in the broader OCW/MOOC movements and their staunchest supporters.

One final issue needs to be raised before concluding a discussion of the problem of pedagogy. Surely, we must recognize that everyone does not learn in the same manner or at the same pace. In this light, there are very real advantages to online forms of education such as those offered by MOOCs. More specifically, even though most MOOCs are typically offered in a synchronous environment, there are still numerous opportunities for learners to proceed at their own pace, focusing on what they deem relevant. This is even true of MOOC courses that have ended, but whose materials may remain available online. Availability and flexibility are obvious benefits of the both the MOOC and OCW movements and are not to be taken lightly. In my mind, these advantages are truly transformative and contribute significantly to the democratization of knowledge.

The Problem of Hegemony

Embedded in the power dynamics of the OCW/MOOC movements is a growing recognition of problems related to the domination of knowledge by elite university providers both domestically and abroad. This problem, which I refer to as the problem of hegemony, raises two important considerations: (1) elite universities dominating the expansion of MOOCs as a source of knowledge and influence in the United States, and (2) the possibility of extending forms of cultural colonialism abroad, given that elite Western universities (especially those in the United States) tend to dominate the MOOC landscape.

The notion that elite universities in the United States are dominating the MOOC movement domestically is increasingly evident in the way only a handful of the wealthiest universities have emerged to lead the MOOC movement. I reference the likes of Columbia, Harvard, MIT, Penn, Yale, and Stanford, among a small group of other highly regarded universities which have more or less come to define the movement. Along these lines, Carnegie Mellon University, another well-funded, elite private university, has been a leader in developing sophisticated cognitive science-based online education tools, thus strengthening the potential of online education innovations such as MOOCs. CMU's Open Learning Initiative, for example, focused on a smaller set of courses by comparison to the Harvard/MIT edX collaboration, but CMU did so in order to emphasis technologically advanced modes of teaching and learning. Using advances in cognitive science and building on its strength in engineering, CMU spent roughly $500,000 to $1 million per course, incorporating such learning tools as "cognitive tutors, virtual laboratories, group experiments, and simulations" (Atkins, Brown, and Hammond 2007, 12). MIT and Harvard similarly invested large sums of money in developing the joint edX initiative, with each university kicking in $30 million to launch the initiative.

When one considers the amount of funding necessary to develop a significant list of meaningful and massive open courses, it becomes easier to understand why the wealthiest universities have come to dominate the OCW/ MOOC arena. As a consequence of financial concerns, among other considerations, many institutional leaders working at public colleges and universities tend to adopt a "wait and see" approach, as a study by the University of Pennsylvania's Alliance for Higher Education and Democracy (AHEAD) reported in April 2014.

The domination of elite universities leads to their own professors assuming front stage in the world of MOOC superstardom. The best example perhaps is Michael Sandel, a political philosopher at Harvard who has achieved rock star status in countries such as South Korea and China (see chapter 2). Even at Harvard, his course on "Justice" has attracted some of the largest enrollments in the history of the university. However, it was Sandel's "JusticeX" course (the online recorded version developed by edX) that helped to fuel early opposition to MOOCs, arising from the Department of Philosophy at San Jose State University. JusticeX was to be offered by SJSU as part of a collaboration forged between edX and California State University, of which SJSU represents one campus (this is a separate issue from problems at SJSU related to Udacity's efforts to offer lower division and remedial courses).

At the heart of the criticism of faculty in SJSU's Department of Philosophy was a critique of elitism and the potential for professors such as Sandel to dominate knowledge dissemination in the form of the university course. SJSU philosophy faculty saw this as a basic assault on the public university and its diverse constituencies. Their concerns were conveyed in a letter addressed to Professor Sandel, dated April 13, 2013. The letter captures one of the basic problems of the expanding MOOC movement at the time—the potential for domination of public institutions by elite privates. Because it is such a powerful and concise indictment of MOOCs, I offer key passages from the letter here:

> First, what kind of message are we sending our students if we tell them that they should best learn what justice is by listening to the reflections of the largely white

student population from a university like Harvard? Our very diverse students gain far more when their own experience is central to the course and when they are learning from our own very diverse faculty, who bring their varied perspectives to the content of courses that bear on social justice.

Second, should one-size-fits-all vendor-designed blended courses become the norm, we fear that two classes of universities will be created: one, well-funded colleges and universities in which privileged students get their own real professor; the other, financially stressed private and public universities in which students watch a bunch of video-taped lectures and interact, if indeed any interaction is available on their home campuses, with a professor that this model of education has turned into a glorified teaching assistant. Public universities will no longer provide the same quality of education and will not remain on par with well-funded private ones. Teaching justice through an educational model that is spearheading the creation of two classes in academia thus amounts to a cruel joke.

In addition to issues of university stratification linked to the ways in which MOOCs were being expanded, other concerns relating to faculty labor also arose within the context of the SJSU criticism, including the possible deskilling of academic labor alluded to by the above reference to a professor becoming a "glorified teaching assistant." I return to this matter in a subsequent section of this chapter focused on the problem of faculty labor.

Gianpiero Petriglieri, writing for the *Harvard Business Review* Blog Network, nicely captured the concerns raised here in a piece titled "Let Them Eat MOOCs," noting that "MOOCs can be used as a cost-cutting measure in already depleted academic institutions and become another weapon against battered faculty bodies. They may worsen rather than eliminate inequality by providing credentials empty of the meaning and connections that make credentials valuable." Petriglieri went on to add, "Worst of all, they may become a convenient excuse for giving up on the reforms needed to provide broad access to affordable higher education. The traditional kind, that is, which for all its problems still affords graduates higher chances of employment and long-term economic advantages." Here, Petriglieri highlighted one of the most significant of all MOOC criticisms—the idea that MOOCs often are envisioned by political figures and policy makers as an *alternative* to adequately funding public higher education systems. Bonnie Stewart (2013), writing for *Inside Higher Ed*, raised this issue as well: "So we need to be wary of bringing in MOOCs to prop up overstretched institutional systems, as California is doing. We particularly need to be wary of invoking MOOCs to deliver on the mythology of education as access to betterment; as a proverbial hand up."

The problem is not the tool—the MOOC—but how the use of that tool has come to be defined as a cost-savings measure, arguably at the expense of low-income and working-class students who are more likely to attend the nation's community colleges and public universities. To put it another way, a new creative tool—think of the MOOC as a plowshare—is being used as a sword.

There is a perception of high quality associated with MOOCs, largely because they are offered by elite universities and often led by rock-star professors. This perception of high quality undergirds the vision of the MOOC as a solution to a particularly vexing problem: lack of adequate funding for public higher education.

The growing role of universities such as Harvard and MIT in spreading course-related knowledge throughout the world through the OCW and MOOC movements highlights another facet to the problem of hegemony—the specter of global domination. I tend to see such domination as holding the potential to spread complex forms of cultural colonialism through course-related knowledge diffusion. This aspect of the MOOC movement not only enables elite institutions in the United States to possibly dominate global higher education markets but also poses the possibility of furthering U.S. economic and cultural interests.

Advocates of OCW and MOOCs often address the courses' potential to serve the needs of teachers and students in many of the world's less developed regions. This speaks to another layer associated with issues of power and knowledge; that is, one must ask who is likely to be the producers of OCW/MOOC course knowledge and who is likely to be the user? I already discussed how elite universities and professors working at them have become dominant in the U.S. context, but the same is likely to occur in the context of an increasingly globalized higher education marketplace. At this point it seems fairly obvious—given their global brands—that elite U.S. universities and others mostly in the Western world will dominate such globalized landscapes.

Many OCW/MOOC advocates talk about the democratization of knowledge and the idea that anyone with a computer and Internet connection has the opportunity to produce knowledge content such as course materials. But this commonly conveyed idea ignores the reality that one must somehow establish an audience. And in the world of university course production, it certainly is quite advantageous to have a university brand such as Harvard, MIT, or Penn connected to one's MOOC.

Another facet to the hegemony of MOOCs and globalization is the reality that the vast majority of OCW course materials are in English, a finding noted by the Organisation for Economic Co-operation and Development in their important report *Giving Knowledge for Free: The Emergence of Open Educational Resources* (2007). As the report highlighted, "The vast majority of OER [OCW] are in English and tend to be based on Western culture. This limits the relevance of the materials for non-English, non-Western settings. There is a risk that language barriers and cultural differences may consign less developed countries to the role of consumers of OER [OCW] rather than contributors to the expansion of knowledge" (2007, 104–105). Although the report's comments address mainly open educational resources and by implication OCW, the same basic problem applies to MOOCs.

In April 2013, Ry Rivard published a provocative piece in *Inside Higher Ed* titled, "The World Is Not Flat." He of course was challenging claims made by Thomas Friedman, who had by this time come out as a big fan of the MOOC movement, describing it in revolutionary terms (Friedman 2013). Rivard, though, raised some counterpoints to Friedman's "flattened world" argument, pointing out that "Online higher education is increasingly hailed as a chance for educators in the developed world to expand access and quality across the globe. Yet it may not be quite so easy. Not only does much of the world not have broadband or speak English, but American-made educational material may be unfit for and unwanted in developing countries." His assertion was based on discussions with academics working in the area of online distance education and OER. Rivard went on to explain that the experience of such scholars raises questions about the MOOC "craze" and its "utopian vision"— "this goal of 'democratizing education' using technology"—and the idea that we don't need brick-and-mortar universities much anymore. Rivard saw this rhetoric "gaining popular appeal among investors, some professors, pundits, politicians and the public." However, as he noted, scholars were beginning to wonder if a one-directional transfer of course materials and knowledge "from the rich north to the poor south" might contribute to a new wave of "intellectual neo-colonialism." Here I might add that this transfer originates not only from the "rich north," but from the richest of the rich north—Harvard, MIT, Penn, Stanford, Yale, and so forth. This is a serious problem if superstar professors from elite universities are to represent U.S.-based understandings of the world at a global level. As SJSU philosophy professors astutely noted, the views of such professors do not represent the range of points of view in academe, nor of the broader society in general.

Another side to the one-directional spread of course materials and knowledge is the potential to utilize MOOCs for identifying global talent to be recruited to the United States, thus furthering brain drain from less resourced regions of the world. In a talk included in William Bowen's 2013 book *Higher Education in the Digital Age*, Daphne Koller offered insight into the thinking of some MOOC advocates:

> Another benefit to opening our doors up to the world is that, again from a selfish perspective, there is unique talent in Mongolia, in Ghana, in Bangladesh— students who achieve perfect scores in some of our most challenging courses. This gives us the opportunity to recruit and identify some of the world's best talent to come to our institutions and enhance our own talent pool and the mix of student that we teach. (155)

To give Koller proper credit, she at least acknowledged the "selfish" nature on her thinking. But she should not be let off the hook for failing to recognize an alternative global possibility for which MOOCs and Internet-based interactions in general might play a role—that is, the opportunity for strengthening the ideals of global citizenship and promoting a more win-win vision of the global flow of people and ideas, perhaps by considering the possibilities of brain circulation. Unfortunately, she fell into an all-too-common pattern of framing educational innovation in terms of furthering U.S. economic hegemony.

In light of the likely dominance of the MOOC movement by leading universities mostly operating in Western nations, what are the implications for less developed nations, which no doubt often find themselves in need of foreign higher education services? I find Edward Said's work helpful and compelling in addressing this concern. Said wrote about the ways in which empire-building still occurs within the contemporary context, but is accomplished less through military domination and more through cultural penetrations. "Ideological combat" is the primary tactic of the modern imperialist enterprise, suggesting that winning over minds is as important today as was conquering physical space in the past. As Said argued, "For reasons that are partly embedded in the imperial experience, the old divisions between colonizer and colonized have re-emerged in what is often referred to as the North-South relationship, which has entailed defensiveness, various kinds of rhetorical and ideological combat, and a simmering hostility that is quite likely to trigger devastating wars—in some cases it already has" (1993, 17).

As my discussion of Foucault earlier in this chapter suggested, the production of knowledge and truth is hardly a neutral activity; knowledge production is tied to power, and various individuals and groups are engaged in efforts to assert their own version of reality. If the global world of the MOOC is primarily shaped by universities in the wealthiest nations, then it seems reasonable to expect that the forms of knowledge and understanding represented by various course materials will reflect the cultural locales from which such materials derive. This is a somewhat subtle but pernicious form of cultural domination and needs to be called into question. We cannot simply accept MOOCs as neutral representations of the world. Instead, we must critique them for the cultural bias and limited conceptions of social reality they potentially convey. Unmasking the ways in which knowledge and power operate culturally is critical to creating a more democratic space for diverse forms of online education, including the world of the MOOC.

The need for a more critical analysis of MOOCs and their global implications is made all the more relevant by initiatives on the part of providers such as Coursera, which in April 2014 announced its commitment to expand its worldwide offerings, detailing how it was forming partnerships around the world. One of the partnerships noted by the for-profit company included efforts to recruit volunteers to participate in a "global translator community" to work on creating subtitle translations of various lectures. As Danya Perez-Hernandez (2014) noted, "The company now offers courses with subtitle translations in 13 foreign languages, with Chinese, French, and Spanish among the most popular. The company says only 40 percent of the people who take its courses live in English-speaking countries." Of course, there is much good that might come from such an enterprise. But at the same time, the opportunity for further inserting a U.S.-dominated worldview clearly exists.

The Problem of Diversity

Criticism of SJSU's collaboration with edX, which initially proposed that the Department of Philosophy adopt Sandel's "JusticeX" course, was one of the first public instances in which the MOOC movement faced indictments relating to what I see as the problem of diversity. By the term "diversity," I refer to an array of diverse social identities that learners have and bring to the learning experience, including online education environments. As countless research studies have demonstrated, a learner's social identity is fundamental to how she or he approaches learning in a wide range of contexts, whether working individually or collaboratively (T. C. Howard 2003; Ladson-Billings 1995). I see the lack of attention to social identities, and diversity more broadly, as a major indictment of the MOOC/OCW movements.

Recall that the philosophy faculty in their letter of protest to Sandel pointed to problems associated with the diverse students of SJSU being required to watch recorded lectures designed to engage the predominantly White student population of Harvard. They questioned how a course focused on justice that essentially ignored the cultural backgrounds and experiences of the diverse SJSU students could ultimately strengthen their understanding of the topic. Indeed, requiring them to participate in such a blended course was likely to further instill in them the inequities of the world—with the privileged students of Harvard getting real professors and the SJSU students watching recorded versions of Harvard's rock-star professors. The fact that few if any MOOC advocates raised these concerns in the first few years of the movement is rather disconcerting. In reviewing much of the OER and OCW research literature, the same charges could be made against advocates of those movements as well. Why then is there such a lack of awareness or commitment to the diversity implications of the OER, OCW, and MOOC movements, especially among their biggest advocates?

In defense of OER/OCW supporters, there has been discussion of issues of economic disadvantage. The discussion though mostly centers on the global reach of OER/OCW and how advancing the ideals of the knowledge commons might benefit the poorest peoples and regions of the world. This indeed has been a concern of many knowledge commons scholars and advocates, as was noted in the previously mentioned OECD report, *Giving Knowledge for Free* (2007). However, while they have paid attention to issues of economic inequality—essentially, class-rooted concerns (no doubt having racial, ethnic, and gendered implications)—they mostly ignored the many other ways that power and privilege play out in social and educational arenas, serving at times to further marginalize diverse individuals and groups. To put it another way, beyond the challenge of assisting learners in the poorest nations of the world and assisting students at under-funded U.S. universities, there is little to no recognition that within countries, including the United States, there are widespread ethnic, racial, and gendered patterns of inequality across a variety of sectors, including in terms of educational access and attainment. There are also significant data pointing to forms of inequality being enacted in the context of in-class and out-of-class learning environments. Colleges and universities pay great attention to the latter forms of inequality, but who addresses these issues in the context of a MOOC?

The problem of diversity is particularly compelling given the claims OCW and MOOC advocates make about their concern for expanding democracy, mostly by promoting a world with equal access to knowledge and information. Indeed, MOOCs are praised for their potential to revolutionize higher learning, to challenge the basic structure of academe and curricula delivery systems. MOOC enthusiasts hail the benefits in terms of their ability to "lift more people out of poverty," to "enable us to reimagine higher education" (Friedman 2013), and to "knock down campus walls" (Lewin 2012b). MOOCs are seen as knitting "together education, entertainment (think gaming) and social networking" (Pappano 2012), and providers, including Coursera, edX, and Udacity, boast of their plans to serve millions of students worldwide (Lewin 2013). But mostly absent from this discussion of the transformative potential of the MOOC, and the broader OCW movement, is a body of work that addresses teaching and learning in the context of societies increasingly defined as global multicultural spaces (Banks 2010; Rhoads and Szelényi 2011). Such societies tend to exhibit a variety of diversity challenges largely ignored by the present-day MOOC and OCW movements. In the world of social struggle, if you're not part of the solution then there stands a pretty good chance that you're part of the problem. As the late Howard Zinn once put it: "You can't be neutral on a moving train."

A variety of issues must be considered relative to diversity and MOOCs, including the digital divide and inequities experienced by lower-income and underrepresented ethnic and racial minorities. Also, issues related to promoting meaningful cross-cultural interaction should be examined. For example, research suggests that students of all races may feel heightened anxiety and discomfort when interactions across race become guarded and tense; in the context of MOOCs delivered to users around the world, there is great likelihood that conversations—regardless of course content—might arise relative to cultural differences. Therefore, it is critical for online educators to facilitate diversity-related initiatives that encourage students' intergroup understanding and pluralistic orientation (Engberg and Hurtado 2011). Race is only one of several key factors that shape social identities and influence the learning experience, with others such as ethnicity, gender, socioeconomic status, physical ability, sexuality, and age also having an impact. Furthermore, various combinations of social identities result in complex social positions best understood through an approach introduced by scholars such as Kimberle Crenshaw (1991) and described as intersectionality. Identity-related influences may become more problematic in specific educational contexts or relative to particular forms of course content. Gender, for example, may demand a deeper analysis and understanding relative to learning environments associated with MOOCs in the so-called STEM fields (science, technology, engineering, and mathematics), given the broad underrepresentation of women and widespread reports of hostile learning environments in these fields.

Research by Di Xu and Shanna Jaggers (2014) focusing on performance gaps between online and face-to-face learning further supports some of the points here. For example, they found that Black students, males, and students with lower levels of academic preparation all evidence lower performance levels in online education settings.[6] They also reported differences in academic subject areas, noting in particular that students in the social sciences and the applied professions (business, law, and nursing) tended to perform more poorly in online courses. Xu and Jaggers explained the gaps this way: "Perhaps these subject areas require a high degree of hands-on demonstration and practice, making it more difficult for instructors to create effective online materials, activities, or assignments. Or perhaps the learning process in these subject areas requires intensive student-instructor interactions and student-student discussions" (652). Although their research focused on online courses more generally and not MOOCs specifically, their findings nonetheless raise important concerns relative to student background characteristics and performance across different content areas.

Diversity concerns in the context of online learning may arise in other ways as well. Andrea Press and Francesca Tripodi (2014) pointed out that online forums and anonymous message boards at times facilitate "the expression of extreme viewpoints, without the usual constraints provided by the norms of civil discourse." They noted that such online environments "have become an important part of a larger system that normalizes misogyny," pointing out as well that mass murderer Elliot Rodger frequently visited the online message board PUAHate, "where users employed extremely misogynistic language." Similarly, Alec Couros (2008, 2009) has noted the potential for social networking sites to be used for predation, bullying, slander, and harassment, calling on educators to be more proactive and intentional toward ensuring a certain level of student safety and comportment. Given this reality, is it hard to imagine that in the context of MOOCs and a variety of online learning environments stressing social interaction, misogynistic—or racist, classist, heterosexist, ethnocentric—comments will arise? In their MRI-funded study of MOOCs and learner motivation and completion rates, Yuan Wang and Ryan Baker (2014) reported that negative commentary emerging in the context of MOOC online forums can have a substantial impact on the learning environment. Although they did not specifically identify hostile or hate speech in their discussion of "negativity," the point is that online forums and discussion boards have the potential to facilitate such forms of expression and that this reality has not been adequately considered by MOOC advocates.

Certainly, I am not suggesting that online speech in the context of a course should be suppressed. What I am suggesting is that it needs to be pedagogically addressed. So, what is the responsibility of MOOC providers to offer a certain level of instructional support in order to encourage respectful learning environments? Such concerns ought to be considered in structuring the various types of learning experiences associated with online teaching and learning platforms likely to be used in MOOCs, especially xMOOCs. To ignore diversity concerns and the potential for hurtful speech to arise in the context of MOOC-related social learning environments is likely to further reinforce inequities and marginality.

The MOOC movement, examined as an innovation in distance education, is deeply informed by the research literature aiming to better serve adult learners, including long-standing trends arising from the Chautauqua adult education movement (Scott 1999). Distance education programs have long aimed to reach a wide range of adult learners, but criticisms have arisen concerning a lack of sensitivity and attention to a range of diversity attributes of learners. For example, Allan Lauzon (1999, 2000) argued that distance education is market-driven, resulting in the promotion of dominant ideologies. Lauzon maintained that in order to be sensitive to the diversity of learners, education must be "*process*-oriented, not *product*-oriented" (2000, 68). In seeking to promote diversity in online education programs, Alan Holzl (1999) advocated a constructivist learning environment, taking advantage of a diverse student population by incorporating their perspectives into course learning outcomes. He further posited that discussion boards and online communications can be more effective for student communications and collaborative learning when efforts are made to limit biases commonly experienced in traditional classroom interactions. The criticism here applies not only to xMOOCs but to cMOOCs as well, given that the arguments advanced by the likes of Lauzon and Holzl are rarely recognized in the context of the connectivist ideals of MOOC teaching and learning. Indeed, the reimagining of teaching and learning from a connectivist standpoint tends to ignore the reality that culture plays a major role in shaping educational environments and that students bring particular cultural backgrounds to their learning experiences (T. C. Howard 2003; Ladson-Billings 1995). As MOOCs continue to attract a diversity of learners from across the globe, it remains to be seen how diversity will be incorporated into various teaching and learning processes as well as accounted for as part of evaluating learning outcomes associated with particular MOOCs. The problem of diversity constitutes a significant barrier to the success of the MOOC movement in the coming years.

I am not arguing that MOOCs cannot be significant contributors in advancing diversity. My point is that from the beginning of the movement through 2014, the discourse surrounding MOOCs largely has ignored diversity issues. There are a number of changes that could take place with regard to better addressing diversity, including MOOC course designers explicitly posting clear expectations about course participants embracing nondiscriminatory language and commentary in course-related conversations. Also, major players in the MOOC movement, such as foundation officers and administrative personnel at MOOC providers, should publicly acknowledge and support the importance of advancing diversity issues for MOOC-related activities and projects.

The Problem of Faculty Labor

Early on in the MOOC movement it became apparent that some of the biggest advocates of MOOCs saw recorded lectures from elite superstar professors as a way of expanding college access through an economy-of-scale approach to teaching. Bill Gates was perhaps one of the most vocal supporters of this idea. An article in the *Chronicle of Higher Education*, published in the fall of 2013, captured a bit of his thinking. Gates noted that the typical professor was likely to have a difficult time competing against the quality of lectures coming from top professors, rendering the traditional lecture somewhat antiquated. As Gates explained, "The quality of those lectures, as they go through the competitive process, will be extremely good. . . . No individual performance is likely to come up to that level" (Mangan 2013). The article went on to note that Gates was aware that "many faculty members felt threatened by suggestions that their lectures could be outsourced to professors at elite institutions." As Gates acknowledged, "Of course it's quite controversial, what software can take over, but once you get a great pool of lectures out there that incorporate problem solving and drill practice, this frees up time" (Mangan 2013). One can see in his comments hints of a foundationalist vision of knowledge. He, for example, spoke of knowledge acquisition as a matter of "drill practice"—perhaps he had in mind the mass of students attending the under-resourced colleges and universities likely to be required to enroll in MOOCs. Is one to presume that higher levels of knowledge exploration and acquisition—the kind that involves students actively engaging in the creation of knowledge, often in conversation with their professors—are to be reserved for Ivy League students? And if many classrooms as we presently know them are to be converted to some modified version of a MOOC, a hybrid of sorts relying on OCW/MOOC digitized lectures and materials, what becomes of the professors who previously facilitated those face-to-face classrooms? To put it another way, what are the implications of public university professors being replaced by the star professors of the world, and what does this suggest about the nature of undergraduate education at marginally funded colleges and universities?

Along a similar line of thinking as Gates, Daphne Koller discussed the benefits she saw to the MOOC model, suggesting that MOOCs covering basic introductory subjects could be produced by a few leading universities to be shared around the country with public universities, essentially offering a "backbone" to U.S. higher education (Kamenetz 2013). Her views on the role of the MOOC speak to both the problem of hegemony—in suggesting that a few leading universities ought to offer basic courses for all of U.S. higher education—and the problem of faculty labor, in terms of her willingness to replace the lectures of professors at public universities with recorded lectures from professors at leading universities. The problem with such logic—on the part of both Gates and Koller—is the shortsightedness of their thinking. What is to become of public universities once their faculty are stripped of one of the most basic of professorial roles, control of courses and classrooms? Furthermore, what evidence do we have that professors at elite universities are better lecturers than the faculty populating our most diverse institutions?

In a study of faculty labor issues conducted by my MOOC research group, we examined the discourse surrounding the emergence and advance of the MOOC movement, focusing on key documents published or released from 2008 through the early part of 2014. In all, we examined over two hundred documents, including policy papers, institutional statements and policies, legislative proceedings, press releases, websites, union statements and collective bargaining reports, faculty organizations' reports (e.g. faculty senates, faculty associations, etc.), and journal articles. We also analyzed news coverage from media outlets such as the *Chronicle of Higher Education*, the *New York Times*, and the *Washington Post* among others. Our goal was to better understand key themes in how the MOOC movement was viewed, discussed, and conceptualized relative to the role of the U.S. professoriate. A key finding of the study pointed to a powerful discourse intending to refashion the nature of faculty work for at least a subpopulation of university professors, namely those employed at under-resourced colleges and universities.

In the midst of a dire economic crisis, reduced funding for higher education, and greater openness to online education, MOOCs spread rapidly following their emergence in 2008. Given concerns about how to finance colleges and universities at a level adequate to support student demand, the economy-of-scale benefits seemingly offered by xMOOCs were hard to ignore. Indeed, they appeared to present an ideal solution to the higher education "cost disease" described by William Bowen (2013), who despite years of obstinacy to online education saw some benefits to MOOCs. But to further cement the MOOC movement as a central force in solving higher education's cost-of-access woes, it was also necessary to redefine the nature of faculty work, at least for a segment of the professoriate—that is, faculty members employed at under-resourced colleges and universities. This involved reframing the teaching role of these faculty members by essentially replacing their face-to-face lectures with those of star professors increasingly available for free through digitized platforms such as YouTube.

Deskilling Faculty Labor

My research in this area draws on the thinking of Harry Braverman (1974), who in his classic work *Labor and Monopoly Capital* analyzed how capitalist production systems strip workers of basic rights by lowering the level of skill required to perform their labor. Braverman maintained that employers produce goods efficiently by purchasing the labor power of employees at the lowest wage possible. A key strategy for paying a low wage is to reduce the level of skill required to perform particular tasks, with technology often serving as a vehicle for implementing such a strategy. Relative to faculty labor and the MOOC movement, by pushing under-resourced public and private universities to rely on MOOCs taught by professors at elite universities, these financially strapped institutions may effectively reduce the skill level required of faculty. In the context of a MOOC-supported blended course (also described as a hybrid course), faculty assume the role of "glorified teaching assistant," as the philosophy faculty at SJSU astutely noted. Furthermore, future hiring efforts aimed at supporting lower-division and introductory courses could potentially focus not on hiring more faculty but instead employing graduate students in such roles, given that instruction in such a system would now be farmed out to star professors employed elsewhere. Thus, by reducing the skill level required to support instruction at a public university, countless dollars are likely to be saved both by replacing faculty with teaching assistants and by reducing the overall size of the faculty. With a smaller faculty, the university also becomes that much easier to manage in that both senior and mid-level administrators no longer must contend with an empowered faculty voice on campus.

Braverman's work thus helps to shed light on what I see as the problem of faculty labor. But I would be remiss if I failed to note that the MOOC movement is not entirely to blame for the assault on faculty work. In some sense, it is simply a symptom of a larger problem—with the primary issue being a lack of commitment to adequately funding meaningful forms of higher learning at a mass level. Given this lack of commitment, it is easier to understand how high-tech educational innovations such as MOOCs captured the attention of so many politicians and policy makers seeking to "Taylorize" higher education (Mirrlees and Alvi 2014; Rees 2014).

A similar argument about the role of online education and technology as a strategy for deprofessionalizing the professorate was offered by David Noble (2001) in his book *Digital Diploma Mills: The Automation of Higher Education.* Noble argued that a certain fixation exists between modernized notions of education reform and automation. This is especially true of universities and university reform, where a kind of preoccupation with automation, typically translated into computerized methods of teaching and learning, often drives efforts to reduce costs by elevating efficiency. Noble traced how implementation of the 1920s correspondence course reflected the same arguments later made about early forms of online education: Namely, that it was a more efficient version of education that also enabled learners to get personalized attention and work at their own pace. This line of reasoning for Noble was more or less a masquerade for offering a second-rate version of the university course by also degrading the work of university instructors. This strategy arguably enables universities to create a more casual, low-level workforce that can more easily be manipulated and exploited.

From Noble's perspective, blind faith in technology drives university decision making aimed at automatizing significant facets of the higher education enterprise, including the most crucial of activities: teaching. By employing high technology to record and digitize the work of faculty, colleges and universities potentially minimize their costs while claiming to offer an equivalent version of the university course experience. Once a faculty member's teaching—often understood as a set of course materials and recorded lectures—is fully commoditized, it may be reproduced again and again. Such strategies, in addition to the faculty labor issues they raise, including copyright concerns, run the risk of dehumanizing the teaching and learning experience in a form of technology-based utopianism. The administratively driven automation of faculty teaching, combined with the casualization of the professorate through reliance on part-timers, further reduces the professionalism of university teachers. Thus, Noble's argument about automation being used to deprofessionalize faculty parallels to a great extent Braverman's critique of deskilled labor. In the end, higher education costs are likely to be reduced, but arguably so is the overall quality of the student learning experience.

The potential problem of labor exploitation relative to online education primarily hinges on the ability of postsecondary institutions to hire lower-level instructors to offer such courses under the university's regular brand. MOOCs, however, offer additional dimensions to the potential exploitation of faculty by producing courses at a massive level, reproducing them cheaply by heavy reliance on digitized materials (this also involves voiding faculty copyright claims) and perhaps most significant, reassigning faculty lecturers to more of a teaching assistant role while professors at leading universities offer course development and recorded OCW lectures.

A key facet to the exploitation of faculty labor involves a struggle over copyright and ownership of course-related materials, including syllabi and recorded lectures. For the university to be the efficient automated machine described to some extent by Noble and implicated by Braverman's notions of monopoly capital, it must win the battle over ownership to the creative work of professors. This necessitates defining faculty as employees and their creations as employee-produced commodities. Of course, such claims fly in the face of ideals associated with academic freedom and principles advanced by the American Association of University Professors, a matter I return to in the final chapter.

In addition to the struggle between universities and the professorate, faculty may also be torn by the clash of democratic ideals: those of the knowledge commons and those relating to faculty labor rights. I say much more about this in the concluding chapter when I highlight some of the practical concerns deriving from the MOOC movement.

In some ways, my analysis here runs the risk of sounding like the arguments offered by the machine-smashing Luddites of the early 1800s who tried to ruin labor-saving machines in order to preserve jobs and protect their artisanship (Morris and Stommel 2014). With such potential accusations hanging in the air, I need to be crystal clear. There is no strong evidence that xMOOCs are an improvement as substitutes for face-to-face courses. There is also no research that has adequately examined the implications of displacing faculty at under-resourced colleges and universities from the role of lecturer to the role of discussion leader. Furthermore, there is no research that adequately examines the overall impact on students and a student body when they are required to take an xMOOCs as a substitute course. Clearly, more research is needed before taking such dramatic steps as refashioning the nature of the teaching role of professors. Again, I am not suggesting that xMOOCs do not work or that we do not have solid evidence of their educational contribution. As I have noted in chapter 3, the MRI research has shown some positive results for xMOOCs, especially when offered as additive preparatory courses for incoming college students. But when it comes to determining the best role of xMOOCs as a form of educational innovation, there is need for deeper and more rigorous research. Future research should not only focus on student learning outcomes relative to a particular MOOC; it also must evaluate the organizational implications of restructuring teaching and learning.

Concluding Thoughts

In addressing five key problems related to MOOCs, my goal is to dig deeper into this important movement in order to develop critical insights. Such insights are useful in charting a course for the future, as I have no doubt that MOOCs and OCW are here to stay, in some manner or form. Just what form MOOCs will take in the coming years remains to be seen, but clearly there are strengths and weaknesses to what we have seen thus far from MOOCs. Obviously, they have much to offer in expanding the knowledge commons and in democratizing the university course. We also see evidence that cMOOCs specifically may work well for professional communities of practice but are difficult to implement. Perhaps cMOOCs are not the best MOOC model for traditional undergraduates, given the self-directed learning quality stressed by connectivism. We also know that xMOOCs hold great potential in terms of addressing a variety of educational needs, from curiosity seeking to skill enhancement and personal development. xMOOCs should not be judged too harshly on the basis of user attrition, as there are a wide range of reasons learners take advantage of them and presumably course completion is not often a goal. Of course, as I have noted in this chapter and elsewhere, I am quite cautious about seeing xMOOCs as substitute courses for traditional classroom instruction, but they seem quite promising as additive preparatory courses.

5

Conclusion

The Future of MOOCs and Higher Learning

In the 2014 revised edition of his book *Why School?*, Mike Rose included a chapter titled "MOOCs and Other Wonders: Education and High-Tech Utopia." The chapter provoked my thinking about a number of MOOC and technology-related issues, pushing me to consider more deeply the meaning of higher learning in an age dominated by technology, or what Rose described as "high-tech utopia." Allow me to draw from the opening passage to Rose's chapter:

> Deep within our cultural history is a faith in the power of technology to cure social problems. Many of our utopian visions—from nineteenth-century social-ist tracts and novels to Silicon Valley's libertarian futurism—are based on technology. That faith is vibrant today, at times idealistic, at times entrepre-neurial, often a blend of the two. Neuroscience will lead to the cure of mental illness and reveal the mystery of consciousness itself. Social media will bring us together across regional and national divides, and the cell phone or tablet computer will provide the platform to lift people in developing countries out of poverty. And . . . online instruction will reduce the cost and improve the quality of education. (147–148)

As Rose went on to argue, overreliance on technology to solve key social prob-lems can be fraught with mistakes and overly simplistic thinking: "The faith in technology can lead to overreach, to a belief that complex human problems can be framed as engineering problems, their social and political messiness fac-tored away" (148).

In some sense, MOOCs represent the sort of unquestioned faith in the power of technology criticized by Rose (2014). The vision of higher learning offered by MOOCs, specifically when deployed as substitutes for face-to-face courses at poorly funded colleges and universities, is suggestive of a type of teaching and learning to be questioned, not reproduced in a massive way. Research tells us that educationally challenged students need greater sources of support, not less. The reality is that MOOCs have been cleverly pushed by entrepreneurs, venture capitalists, high-tech advocates, legislators, policy makers, and efficiency-minded administrators as a quick solution to a serious problem involving the kind of "social and political messiness" to which Rose alluded. MOOCs certainly have a place in higher education and in advancing forms of higher learning, but we need to be cautious in employing them as a quick fix for all sorts of complex and messy problems.

Elizabeth Losh's (2014) *The War on Learning: Gaining Ground in the Digital University* also raises important questions about the role of technology, particularly with regard to teaching and learning in the twenty-first-century university. A central thesis of her book is the "folly of overvaluing innovation," arguing that "MOOCs, badge systems, gamification, iPad distributions, and Second Life grab the headlines by appealing to trends," but "students need models that have been tested, not fads" (236). Losh, a media studies scholar who writes about the field of science, technology, and society (STS), is not opposed to instructional technology per se; she simply prefers a more thoughtful approach to its adoption and implementation as part of viewing education as a process, not a product. In her book, she argued that "success in implementing a new instructional technology depends on having a critical mass of faculty colleagues willing to share their experiences. Such pedagogical communities require there to be enough trust that failures can be assessed honestly and lessons learned can be shared without jealousy and covetousness" (237). Losh's ultimate concern is not to reject the growing power and role of high technology and its influence on teaching and learning but to ask critical questions, such as: How can the digital university "be more inclusive, generative, just, and constructive?" What can be learned from "embodied interactions in the lived experiences" of today's university students and teachers, as opposed to simply giving the university over to the untested ideas and structures of entrepreneurs and venture capitalists? Her defining question reflects a desire to "avoid overestimating machines" as innovative solutions to the challenges of teaching and learning (224). When it comes to the introduction of new technologies into university classrooms, Losh sees the need for faculty and students to be centrally engaged in discussions about what works and doesn't work.

In conducting classroom observations as part of data collection for her book, Losh (2014) observed an experiment in distance learning in which the faculty lecturer appeared only as a "broadcast version" on the classroom screen, while students responded to course content and "clicker quizzes." She offered the following provocative take:

> In that lecture hall, the once-covert war between "us" and "them" had turned into an open battle between "our" technologies and "their" technologies. On one side, we faculty could reset countdown clocks and forgive clicker mishaps, but they had access to wireless networks and mobile telephony. My sensibilities as an educator were assaulted by this spectacle of mutual contempt, but it seemed futile to try to engage anyone present in a conversation about what they were perpetuating and why. (38–39)

The point here is not that face-to-face teaching is good and that recorded lectures are bad; in fact, Losh also observed the same instructor in a face-to-face classroom, noting that "about half of the students . . . were partially engaged" and "only paid attention during the quiz portions of the session" (38). Instead, the point is the ubiquity of technology on both sides—teachers and students—and the lack of critical analysis of the deployment of instructional technology, in both face-to-face classrooms and online ones. Losh sees the tendency to embrace high-tech devices without adequate analysis concerning their impact on students and learning as an outcome of the fixation with trendiness.

Losh targeted what she perceived as a lack of serious attention to the shortcomings of the xMOOC model. To be fair, her analysis mostly ignored cMOOCs, and she gave far greater attention to Coursera's model of the xMOOC than to other versions. Nonetheless, she raised a key point about the meaning of "open" and how significant players in the MOOC movement such as Coursera have stressed "open" mostly as "free," as opposed to embracing what David Wiley defined as "open" in terms of users being able to "reuse, remix, revise, and redistribute" (2013, 138); Wiley's "4Rs" capture the important quality of "shareable" as part of the meaning of open. Losh's point is not a trivial one in that arguably the most empowering facet to the MOOC and OCW movements is the ability for users (typically self-directed users) to have the opportunity to actively engage courses, including refashioning the course content and materials. In stressing the xMOOC model, providers such as Coursera tend to embrace a disempowering form of online instructional design. As she explained, "A course being open for anyone to change and redirect and a course being open for anyone to witness, as long as they are passive spectators in the audience, can connote two very different kinds of educational experiences" (136). Her criticism is analogous to concerns I have raised in chapter 4 relating to the problems of epistemology and pedagogy. The important point for both of us is that although the MOOC movement has potential to advance empowering forms of teaching and learning, the dominant instructional practices of most MOOCs involve significant compromises.

The work of both Rose and Losh highlights the need to dig more deeply into the world of the MOOC and the actual ways in which students may or may not benefit from this recent high-tech educational innovation. After all, innovations ought to be a step forward, not backward, and the impact on students and student learning needs to be central to defining improvement. But research on the impact and implications of MOOCs must extend beyond simply assessing course-related learning outcomes. There are far-reaching organizational implications tied to adopting less face-to-face modes of teaching and learning, and they too must be considered in weighing how best to incorporate MOOCs into a university's curriculum. Again, I am relatively supportive of MOOCs, but we need to develop greater insight into the best ways to use them.

Allow me to offer a basic example capturing one type of organizational problem I see with automating courses, especially lectures, in place of face-to-face contact. Here I turn once again to my undergraduate lecture course at UCLA in the education studies minor, a course typically enrolling eighty students. Every fall semester at the culmination of the course I get six or seven requests from students for letters of recommendation, typically to be used in graduate school applications. I always ask them to send me their resume and make an appointment to meet with me in person. The meeting tends to involve a good deal of informal mentoring, given their limited understanding of the graduate application process. Keep in mind that UCLA is a rather diverse university, and many of the undergraduates with whom I work are first-generation college students with limited understanding of the complexities of higher education and the world of professional careers. The entire process amounts to a good deal of work, and I often must submit letters to several different universities for each student applying to graduate school. Now, what would likely happen to these students and these kinds of interactions if my course were restructured as a MOOC, open to students anywhere in the world, but also to unlimited numbers of UCLA students? Assuming that the face-to-face instruction were replaced by digitally recorded versions of my lectures (a must if the course is to be massive), what would be the likelihood of the UCLA students and I forming the kind of relationship in which they feel comfortable enough to approach me about a letter? I imagine this to be highly unlikely. Furthermore, it is just as unlikely that I would agree to write a letter for a student who is simply a name without a face. To run the risk of being repetitive, I am not opposed to MOOCs as university courses, but I'm concerned about the way we define and frame their use.

In this final chapter, I further develop my analysis of the MOOC movement and the high-tech culture from which it has arisen as a means to strengthen a particular vision of higher learning. I need to be clear, though, in terms of my positioning. I do not intend to take a final shot at high-tech educational solutions and the growing contribution of the Internet and social networks to how we think about teaching and learning. Surely, one can offer a serious critique of the role of high technology in teaching and learning environs without resorting to knee-jerk reactionism bordering on technophobia. Charting a kind of middle ground—involving a merger of sorts between technology and humanism—should not be seen as a compromised position. Instead, I see technological solutions as having great potential to inform learning in today's complex social environments. Such solutions, though, should not be developed and implemented without being informed by critical analyses of power, domination, and inequality. This reflects my basic position that we need to examine social change and educational innovation with an eye to potential inequities arising in the context of so-called solutions.

MOOCs, or some version of them, are here to stay. What we need, then, is to give more serious thought to problems arising in the context of the MOOC movement, being particularly mindful of the ways in which they may place certain populations at a disadvantage. The kind of critical analysis I suggest here is central to the five problems highlighted in chapter 4, focusing on epistemology, pedagogy, hegemony, diversity, and labor, as well as to other key issues raised in chapters 1 through 3.

With the preceding in mind, this chapter first considers how higher learning often is conceptualized in an age of high-tech innovations and Internet-based learning opportunities. I move on to address key practical considerations of MOOCs, first in terms of the broader higher education arena, then in terms of specific issues impacting faculty, and then with regard to the role of national- and state-level organizations. Finally, I conclude the chapter and book with closing thoughts and ideas to ponder relative to MOOCs, high technology, and higher learning.

Higher Learning in an Age of High Technology

Despite contradictions and differences of opinion on the role of technology in teaching and learning, it is hard to deny that the MOOC movement has had a major influence on how higher learning is conceptualized. The strength of the MOOC movement rests with its key contribution to expanding the broader OER and OCW movements, enabling learners around the world to gain access to forms of knowledge typically reserved for students formally enrolled in courses at brick-and-mortar colleges and universities. At a surface level, it is hard to criticize the democratic quality of the movement. But despite the democratic potentialities of MOOCs, there are serious issues to reconcile, including the tension between faculty creating and sharing course materials in an open manner while at the same time protecting the value of their labor. Other issues also arise, such as the degree to which a small group of providers might eventually dominate the MOOC arena and what a reasonable response might look like.

For critical humanists such as myself, technology can sometimes obfuscate the potential of higher education to spur social and political empowerment in that the deployment and utilization of high-tech modalities and devices may distract teachers and learners from the liberating possibilities of higher learning. High technology tends to suggest technical solutions to society's problems, while larger political and cultural influences get ignored; a similar point was made by Rose (2014) with regard to high-tech educational reforms. The MOOC movement offers a case in point in that massive online courses were presented as a technical solution potentially enabling greater numbers of students to gain access to higher education. But who were the students to be targeted by this new high-tech innovation? They were, and largely continue to be, students occupying under-funded colleges and universities—mostly public institutions but some privates as well—or populations of learners mostly locked out of higher education's doors. Working from the perspective of critical humanism, we are confronted with this question: Why should we accept strategies to create alternative online forms of higher education for the masses, while preserving the most enriching face-to-face environments for those with greater financial means? MOOCs are referenced as the latest high-tech educational solution, hailed as transformative, revolutionary, and innovative, but for whom are they beneficial and under what circumstances are they effective? The past few years of experimentation suggest they are not ideal as substitute courses, but may be quite helpful as additive learning opportunities intended to elevate basic knowledge and skills. The latter use may contribute in significant ways to strengthening higher education access by better preparing students for particular types of coursework, such as enhancing math skills at the start of study in STEM or related fields. We also must recognize their value for populations having no access at all to university courses, yet critical questions still need to be raised, such as the problem of hegemony.

Education more than ever must incorporate serious questions about the role of technology not only in the context of teaching and learning but in terms of a critique of society more broadly. To borrow again from Rose (2014), we must take issue with a history of blind faith in the power of technology to solve pressing social problems. Along these lines, Rose questioned the hyper-fascination with MOOCs, highlighting what he described as "the humanistic argument": the idea that "education involves more than watching a lecture on a computer, even if enhanced with options for interaction. What about the spontaneous give-and-take between teacher and student? What about the teacher's in-the-moment assessment of classroom dynamics? This concern, of course, reflects a broader tension of our time between electronic connection versus human touch" (152–153).

Computer- and Internet-based interactions and applications have useful roles to play in advancing teaching and learning environments, but perhaps they are best viewed as supplements to direct interaction and engagement with face-to-face teachers—especially when considering the needs of struggling students with less-than-ideal educational backgrounds. Avatars may give well-conceived, insightful, digitally recorded lectures, but the professors who develop the knowledge to construct such lectures in the first place should not remain Oz-like characters in the latest teaching and learning revolution intended for the masses. Again, I find Rose's insights helpful: "When will we stop this distracting and, in fact, expensive worship of the new technological system or device and settle into the less enthralling but more substantial recognition that MOOCs—or any other wonder, from digital games to the most recent statistical procedure—will only be as useful as the thinking about their use, the depth of learning we want to achieve, the kind of education we want to foster" (160–161). To treat high-tech educational solutions such as MOOCs as the "magic bullet" or "quick fix," as Rose posited, only derails the very real task of advancing educational access for all students desiring high-quality higher learning. We can no longer afford to claim that we can no longer afford meaningful forms of higher education. MOOCs and related online education technologies surely can supplement quality education, but they should not be the replacement product pushed on our least advantaged learners.

It is quite telling to me that one of the greatest capitalists in U.S. history— Bill Gates—also is one of the biggest advocates for forms of education that at times can be disempowering. Gates has powered his way to the front and center of educational reform, stressing his own particular version of social reality defined in terms of data-driven analytics and computerization. In pointing to the power of software and computerization to provide essential feedback to online learners engaged in a variety of educational "drills," he highlights the epistemological limitations of his particular vision of knowledge; one gets the sense that knowledge is transferred to students through repetition and that computers and software serve to guide students as they progress. Certainly, there are forms of understanding aligned with this vision—such as solving a basic statistical problem with limited complexity and a small range of possible correct answers. Equally certainly, there are complex forms of knowledge and understanding not so easily programmed as computerized feedback using the latest in artificial intelligence. Gates's thoughts on knowledge and knowledge acquisition stand in direct opposition to the rich and caring discourses stressed by Paulo Freire's humanistic pedagogy.

It is important to recognize here that the MOOC movement depicts to a great extent two differing visions of the massive online course: the original cMOOC and the far more common xMOOC. I see the social learning and connectivist nature of effective cMOOCs as fairly consistent with promoting the sort of democratic and caring dialogues advanced by Freirian pedagogy. However, such courses are difficult to manage as massive enterprises, and they also necessitate a great deal of self-directed behavior on the part of learners. They seem less ideal for traditional college students than for professionals already engaged in a particular field and highly motivated to upgrade their knowledge and skills. Perhaps it is time to acknowledge a hybrid MOOC in which massive enrollment is a goal, but at the same time complex forms of social learning and academic support are also offered to a subpopulation of users. Such a model maintains the ideals of the knowledge commons by making the course and its materials massively open, but at the same time with helpful supplements the course could potentially be used for a targeted group of learners. As I have noted in chapter 1, we might think of this as an *xs*MOOC—a MOOC with extra support; we could also think of this model as a hybrid MOOC, not to be confused with hybrid face-to-face courses utilizing digitized online materials such as previously recorded lectures. Such a model already exists, but as of yet it is not consistently identified. Naming this model may be necessary, though, as the MOOC idea is overly broad and encompasses too much diversity. When I think of xsMOOCs, what comes to mind is Mark Warschauer's study at UC Irvine, in which a massive course—an xMOOC—formed the basis for the curriculum students undertook, but a subpopulation of enrollees was targeted with additional support primarily in the form of incentivization (students were able to enroll in UC Irvine's biology major at an earlier date if they performed well in the Bio Prep MOOC).[1] This model seems far more promising than the pure xMOOC version, at least in terms of promoting higher education access as part of an additive preparatory course.

MOOCs and the Broad Arena of Higher Education

Former Yale University president and Coursera CEO Richard Levin, in an interview from June 2014, offered that "In 10 or 20 years, when we judge the great universities, it will not just be on their research but on the reach of their teaching." As Steve Kolowich (2014a), writing for the Chronicle *of Higher Education*, aptly noted, "That perspective dovetails, of course, with the mission of the company Mr. Levin now leads." It certainly is beneficial to Coursera if university leaders around the world embrace Levin's logic, as many are likely to see Coursera as a well-positioned partner in extending the reach of their university's teaching. However, there remain many barriers to the further expansion of MOOCs and other forms of university-initiated online education, including the reality that growth of the movement is tied to the intellectual work and labor of faculty members, who often are absent from university decisions to further develop online endeavors such as MOOCs. There is also a pressing need to raise more critical concerns about the MOOC movement and its role in higher education, at a minimum to bring a degree of balance to the discussion. Accordingly, in what follows I identify and discuss several practical concerns relating to MOOCs and the broad arena of higher education.

MOOCs as a potential remedy for problems confronting higher education in the twenty-first century must be considered relative to the diversity of the MOOC model, specifically in terms of the different strengths and weaknesses associated with cMOOCs, xMOOCs, and what I call xsMOOCs. MOOCs represent a range of tools—or educational "strategies" (Morris and Stommel 2012)—better at some things than they are at others. Hence, they need to be cautiously applied to particular types of vexing educational problems. This necessarily involves discriminating among the various models.

xMOOCs as a solution to the problems of higher education access, especially when used as substitute courses to serve the least privileged student populations, must be applied in a judicious manner with an eye to a range of educational implications beyond simply specific course-related learning outcomes; in many instances, additional course support should be offered to subpopulations of students in the form of the xsMOOC. There are basic shortcomings associated with xMOOCs largely linked to the limitations of organizing, delivering, and assessing courses and course-related outcomes at a massive level. This version of the MOOC poses a challenge in terms of adopting a sophisticated view of knowledge and often is overly dependent on one-directional forms of pedagogy. Higher learning defined in such a manner does not seem beneficial to the most educationally disadvantaged populations in the United States and around the world. However, as a source of course-related knowledge, xMOOCs may contribute in significant ways and in a manner consistent with the knowledge commons. Accordingly, the high attrition rates associated with xMOOCs ought to be assessed in light of a wide range of user objectives, including the reality that teachers and practitioners alike often use xMOOCs to expand their knowledge and skills with little intent of actually completing a particular course.

Adequate support for student engagement in cMOOC learning environments needs to reflect the levels of technological skill and content-based knowledge one might reasonably expect of particular populations of students. cMOOCs offer important learning experiences not only related to mastering course content but also in terms of various learning outcomes linked to working together in online learning communities. This type of engagement can promote more advanced social networking skills in a manner consistent with the development of collective intelligence. The connectivist learning environments promoted by cMOOCs are likely to be key to future lifelong and continuing education demands in a variety of fields and occupations. Thus, colleges and universities committed to cMOOCs will be better positioned to promote the skills and dispositions increasingly needed in complex professional environments. However, if institutions are to experiment with cMOOCs, they should not assume that all college students (or prospective students) have the prerequisite Internet-based networking skills for generating self-directed and collaborative learning communities. Adequate support must be offered for such efforts to succeed.

MOOCs framed as a revenue-generating or cost-savings strategy need to be rigorously assessed relative to particular organizational contexts and educational objectives. The basic concept of the MOOC is part of the "open" ideals of the Open Educational Resource and Open Courseware movements. "Open" used in the context of MOOCs more or less signifies that courses are to be free and in many cases shareable. Turning MOOCs into revenue-generating schemes involves refashioning them into more traditional online courses and in the process rejects the essence of what constitutes a MOOC. In other words, MOOCs and online education revenue-generating ventures should not be confounded. If higher education institutions desire to generate revenue through online education programs, then the MOOC educational model may not be the best fit. However, if the organizational intent is cost savings in the form of reducing course production costs, then xMOOCs may be an option; again though, caution must be exercised in adopting such a strategy, and a range of organizational outcomes must be analyzed, including the impact on faculty life and overall student learning.

Whether offering cMOOCs, xMOOCs, or xsMOOCs, higher education institutions need to do a better job of addressing issues of student diversity and encourage forms of teaching and learning more likely to promote cross-cultural understanding. The MOOC movement has almost entirely ignored a large body of work in higher education about the impact of diverse social identities on the teaching and learning environment. In committing to MOOCs as an educational option, colleges and universities, including course developers and facilitators, need to be mindful of the ways learning and identity interact and how particular facets of one's social identity may enter into online discussions and group collaborations. For example, MOOC data reveal that the majority of MOOC takers are male. To what extent then do female participants experience a supportive environment for online engagement and learning? To be sure, MOOCs hold the potential to foster more supportive environments than perhaps some of our face-to-face classrooms, given what we already know about the chilly classroom climates female students sometimes face in STEM-related courses. But as it stands now, little has been done with regard to MOOC teaching and learning environments and diversity. We surely need to know more about such issues and enhance MOOC strategies on the basis of the evidence as opposed to relying so heavily on guesswork.

Strategies to counter-balance the domination of elite providers must be considered so as to offer and promote a diversity of knowledge representations in MOOC offerings and course materials. The massively open quality of MOOCs when combined with the realities of globalization raise the potential for a few elite providers (with the most powerful brands) to dominate the world of massive open online education. Although it may be quite valuable to observe lectures from an elite Harvard or Yale professor, every discipline or topical area benefits from considering a wide range of perspectives. Supporters of the MOOC movement and of the knowledge commons more generally need to actively advance strategies to limit institutional hegemony and a limited representation of knowledge. Although it may be hard to imagine formalized mechanisms for countering the influence of elite institutions and superstar professors, informal strategies and organized social movements may have greater likelihood for success. One example comes from the philosophy professors at San Jose State University, who organized a variety of efforts to thwart the imposition of a Harvard-originated xMOOC upon their students.

Sensible policies must be designed and adopted to protect and support faculty engagement in the development and implementation of MOOCs. As I have noted several times throughout this work, considerations of faculty labor often are left out of the MOOC discussion. This is quite problematic given that faculty tend to be the key players involved in the development and proliferation of course content. Although it is noble of faculty members to support the knowledge commons ideals embedded in the MOOC/OCW movements, they also must consider their overall role and obligation to protect the quality of the student learning experience while considering the broad implications MOOCs hold for faculty labor. Given the importance of these concerns to the MOOC movement and to how we conceptualize higher learning, I delve into some of the practical issues of faculty labor more deeply in the next section, including most notably copyright issues and the need for adequate instructional technology support.

Some Practical Considerations Impacting Faculty

Given a deeper understanding of the MOOC movement, including some of the strengths and weaknesses of the various MOOC models, it is helpful to consider specific issues impacting faculty. This is especially important as colleges and universities increasingly seek to develop enriching online educational experiences both for formal and informal learners. In discussing practical issues impacting faculty, I address two particular areas of concern: (1) copyright and intellectual property issues, and (2) instructional technology support and related faculty development.

Copyright and Intellectual Property Issues

A major concern expressed about MOOCs, and related to the faculty labor issues raised in chapter 4, involves complex matters tied to copyright and intellectual property. The issues here extend beyond simply the world of the MOOC, touching the broader OER and OCW movements as well. An argument may be made that although MOOCs hold transformative possibilities in expanding educational opportunities for both formal and informal learners, they do so at the expense of faculty labor. More specifically, the concern is that in allowing their course development and teaching to be fashioned in reusable formats (to be automated in some sense), potentially to be deployed at a massive level, faculty are in essence asked to turn over the rights and interests to their scholarly works, which for their universities may be conveniently defined as employer-supported educational commodities. This is where competing values and interests come together. On the one hand, there are the ideals of the knowledge commons and the inherent value of providing knowledge and information for free, including course materials. On the other hand, when faculty turn over the basic products of their working lives, they leave themselves vulnerable to labor exploitation in that their employers (or other parties) may use their materials over and over again. In certain cases, the university as employer may even negotiate away rights to the materials, offering them to a third-party vendor. Faculty members may be involved in such deals, but it is not clear that they are fully informed of the complex legal implications or that universities have their interests in mind when negotiating third-party agreements. University attorneys are likely to be involved in these kinds of negotiations, but their job is to represent the university and its administration—they do not typically have faculty interests at heart.

A number of scholars have raised key concerns about the need to better protect faculty work involved in the development and production of online courses. Colleen Lye and James Vernon, two faculty members active in the Faculty Association at the University of California, Berkeley, wrote a provocative essay for the *Chronicle of Higher Education* in May 2014. As they explained, "In the rush to online education, faculty members have been signing contracts that abrogate the ownership of their classes, erode their collective interests, and threaten the quality of higher education. No standard (let alone best) practice has yet emerged, and faculty members are largely in the dark about what is at stake." They pointed out that online education, including the world of the MOOC, is a "new frontier" where the "traditional rights of faculty members and the quality of instruction are up for grabs." A concern was expressed that even tenure-track faculty members could become teachers who "work for hire." Lye and Vernon went on to highlight how their university in 2013, without faculty consultation, signed a contract with edX "in a scramble to join the club of private elite universities and private spinoffs . . . developing online-education platforms and course content targeted at underfunded public-education markets." They also noted numerous subunits at their university increasingly involved in online education, including the School of Public Health and the Haas School of Business, questioning the degree to which the university's academic senate could keep up with all the new online developments.

The concerns expressed by Lye and Vernon (2014) principally related to copyright issues and the protection of faculty rights. As they noted, the University of California's existing policy states that all teaching and teaching-related materials, including lectures and lecture notes, are "protected by copyright and the creators of the material have exclusive rights to their uses." However, when universities such as UC Berkeley sign agreements with entities such as edX or Coursera, faculty members involved in course development typically are expected to sign over copyrights or agree to alternative forms of copyright protections. What is not clear is whether faculty members fully understand the implications of such decisions, not only for the individual instructor but for the professoriate more broadly. In terms of the latter point, there are, for example, implications when faculty lose a degree of control over the quality of education offered to students, both at their own campus and throughout higher education generally.

As part of an effort to clarify faculty rights, the Faculty Association at UC Berkeley hired a copyright lawyer to investigate matters further and then offer guidance, particularly in terms of universities laying claim to copyright of faculty-produced course materials and mostly on the grounds that university resources are used to produce such materials. The following was highlighted by Lye and Vernon (2014) in their article:

> When the university claims full ownership of a course, the university is free to re-offer it, revise it, license its use by others, or transfer its ownership to a third party. The university would be able to do that without either seeking the

approval of the instructor who developed the intellectual content of the course, or paying her any additional compensation. In contrast, the instructor would not be able to use the course materials without a license or permission from the university, and could be sued for damages on the grounds of copyright infringement if she did so. The instructor would also be unable to use the course materials to create derivative works. Demanding that faculty members sign over their course copyright is effectively a land grab of the intellectual property and the academic reputation of the instructor.

Clearly, there are serious issues at stake when universities claim copyrights to faculty-produced courses, especially if those courses are to be offered as a form of online education as in the case of MOOCs. As universities continue to view MOOCs as possible cost-saving strategies, it is likely they will invoke their own full or partial ownership of university courses and related course content. Colleges and universities invest heavily in instructional activity and legally have certain claims to employee-produced products. With this in mind, faculty associations, senates, and labor unions should work to clarify and perhaps strengthen the rights of faculty members in order to prevent the exploitation of their labor. A reasonable strategy may be for individual institutions and faculty representatives to develop copyright policies agreeable to both faculty members and their universities through such practices as joint ownership of copyright. But even in terms of the latter, as Lye and Vernon posited, "The university would still be able to offer the course in its original form for as long as it liked or in any number of derivative versions, without consultation or approval by the instructor."

In addition to copyright issues between faculty and universities over MOOC course content and digitized materials such as lectures, there are a host of complex matters emerging relative to the broader world of OER and faculty-produced products. For example, although basic ideals associated with OER and the knowledge commons suggest openness to sharing one's ideas and creations, a concern about protecting faculty labor from commercial exploitation—including exploitation by higher education entities—runs somewhat counter to the democratization of knowledge. Some have argued that faculty interests may be served when they allow others to use their work for noncommercial purposes in the sense that original ideas may be strengthened through their reuse and reapplication. Yet limiting the commercial applications of one's work by others may curtail the spread of new ideas. Along these lines, Richard

Baraniuk (2008) argued that noncommercial licenses serve to limit the advance of knowledge while also undermining nonprofit organizations working in the arena of OER, given the latter's dependence on generating revenue through the reuse of open content. He pointed out how anticommercial practices run contrary to the evolution of the open source software movement in that nonprofits have benefitted from the contributions of for-profit entities. He questioned whether free and open source software endeavors such as Linux and Apache could have developed so successfully "without the value-adding contributions of for-profit companies like Red Hat and IBM" (231). Although the central focus of Baraniuk's discussion is OER, the matters he raised also concern MOOCs, given the likelihood that free course content delivered by professors may be highly reusable, potentially containing commercializable content.

The copyright issues relative to MOOCs are not easy to reconcile. Ultimately, individual professors need to be informed of a range of concerns and options tied to sharing course content and potential tensions between the democratization of knowledge and the exploitation of labor.

New entities emerging to strengthen understanding of copyright issues in a digital age will be critical to supporting further development of the OER, OCW, and MOOC movements while better informing those whose academic labor undergirds these endeavors. For example, the Authors Alliance is a nonprofit group organized to help writers better understand the complexities and tensions associated with reaching larger audiences while at the same time protecting their right to generate revenue. The group's website outlines its basic purpose: "The Authors Alliance embraces the unprecedented potential digital networks have for the creation and distribution of knowledge and culture. We represent the interests of authors who want to harness this potential to share their creations more broadly in order to serve the public good." The Alliance developed a set of key principles for copyright reform, including the following: giving authors more power to decide how to share their works; making it easier to register copyrights and find information about who owns the rights to a work; reaffirming limits on copyright that make it possible for scholars and creators as well as libraries and other cultural institutions to make fair use of material now and in the future; and making sure that copyright remedies and enforcements protect the interests of authors without discouraging creativity (J. Howard 2014). Similar principles are needed to specifically address course-related content and the work of faculty members involved with

MOOCs and other forms of OER/OCW. Faculty unions and associations should be expected to forge such principles as part of further protecting faculty work.

The American Association of University Professors has actively campaigned to protect faculty copyrights, especially in light of the emergence of MOOCs. Speaking at the organization's 2013 annual conference, former AAUP president Cary Nelson warned of the dangers of allowing universities to claim ownership over MOOCs. He saw copyright issues as part of a larger struggle over ownership of intellectual property. As Nelson warned, "If we lose the battle over intellectual property, it's over. . . . Being a professor will no longer be a professional career or a professional identity" and the nature of the work will be more like that of "a service industry" (Schmidt 2013).

The AAUP has urged faculty to get intellectual property right protections in writing, as universities and professors often find themselves on opposing sides in legal disputes over ownership of faculty-produced inventions. In light of the growth of online education, evidenced in part by the rise and expansion of the MOOC movement, faculty teaching-related materials may be up for grabs with university administrators seeking to define course materials as employee-produced commodities to be co-owned by the university. A November 2013 report from the AAUP—"Defending the Freedom to Innovate: Faculty Intellectual Property Rights after Stanford v. Roche"—warned of this interpretation by university administrators and offered the following paragraph as a potential guide to be included in faculty handbooks or collective bargaining agreements:

> The university shall make no claim of ownership or financial interest in course materials prepared under the direction of a faculty member unless the university and faculty member have so agreed in a separate, voluntary agreement. Payment of a financial stipend, use of university resources, or release time to develop course materials shall not be construed by the university as creating a basis for a claim of institutional ownership of such materials, nor shall it be assumed that a work-for-hire relationship exists between the university and the faculty member with regard to the preparation of any such materials.

The report went on to argue that this provision is "especially relevant to the creation of MOOCs, where the use of university resources . . . tends to be greater."

Given concerns relating to faculty rights, including copyright and intellectual property issues, the following are some considerations that must be weighed as faculty members and their home institutions move deeper into the world of the MOOC and online education more generally:

- Faculty senates, unions, and associations need to develop useful guides and principles to assist faculty members in making decisions regarding their engagement with MOOCs.
- Copyright and intellectual property workshops and information sessions should be organized by faculty senates, unions, and associations, as opposed to relying on university legal staff or technology managers to lead such sessions.
- Copyright agreements need to be developed that balance institutional investment and related rights with the rights of faculty to their course-related content and materials.
- Faculty members need to become more assertive in demanding representation in university decision making relative to the development of MOOCs as an educational strategy. Too often such decisions are made absent the voice of professors.
- Faculty senates, unions, and associations should challenge university-initiated efforts to require faculty members to sign agreements in which they essentially allow the university to lay claim to faculty inventions the moment they come into existence (this is known as an "assignment of expectant interests"). Although such policies typically target patentable inventions, the principle established by them could potentially be applied to course-related innovations. The University of California, for example, has adopted such a policy, requiring faculty to sign an agreement assigning the rights to their future inventions to the UC Regents.

These and other points need to be considered if MOOCs are to be pursued in a manner consistent with assuring faculty rights and protections.

Instructional Technology Support and Faculty Development

Assuming adequate protections against the exploitation of faculty labor are in place, practical matters involved in developing and implementing MOOCs must be considered. Given the complexities involved in constructing such learning environments, a key practical concern then becomes offering faculty adequate instructional technology (IT) support and appropriate faculty development opportunities.

Perhaps the biggest challenge to promoting rich learning environments through modalities such as the MOOC is limited faculty knowledge and skill in developing and organizing course-related materials in Internet-based teaching and learning environments. It is one thing to add a few YouTube videos to one's in-class lecture but quite another to develop a series of one's own recorded lectures and link them to a variety of Internet-based resources. Furthermore, developing the kinds of group-based, collaborative online projects consistent with cMOOCs requires understanding a variety of social media sites and their basic functionalities. Along these lines, universities and their various subunits (schools, departments, divisions, etc.) need to provide extensive IT staff to assist faculty both in developing courses and also in advancing their knowledge and skills of various instructional tools.

Strategies for furthering faculty IT competencies ought to include workshops, brown-bag opportunities, and one-on-one meetings with appropriate IT staff. The latter is highly recommended, given that many faculty members may be reluctant to publicly acknowledge their limited IT knowledge in venues like a department, school, or university workshop. Additionally, some Internet-based tools and websites are best explored in a hands-on manner; having IT staff readily available during such exploration can be a major encouragement.

In sampling college and university offerings in the area of MOOC-related workshops, as well as workshops about blended and hybrid forms of course development and instruction, the following list conveys some of the topics typically covered by IT and teaching staff involved in online education:

- Creating blended/hybrid classes
- Teaching online and the role of collaboration
- The basics of Blackboard (or other course platforms)
- Keys to giving recorded lectures
- Grading using online course platforms
- Facilitating online learning communities
- Constructing and implementing peer-graded assignments
- Using Second Life and other virtual worlds (including multi-user domains or MUDs)
- Social media and student-to-student course engagement

- Google applications for education
- Alternatives to PowerPoint presentations, such as Prezi
- Writing e-books
- Smartboards and sympodiums
- Discussion boards and instructor/TA responsiveness
- Automated assessments, quizzes, and tests
- Online learning ecosystems

Of course, this list is far from exhaustive, but it nonetheless offers an inkling of the kinds of workshops and discussions that would be helpful for many faculty members.

In addition to providing faculty with adequate IT support, faculty reward structures must take into account the time and effort needed to develop high-tech instructional practices such as those typically involved with MOOCs. Promotions and reviews involving evaluations of teaching ought to include the opportunity for faculty to highlight their engagement with technology as part of enhancing their instructional skills and abilities. This is not to suggest that all faculty need to become tech-savvy instructors. Instead, those who do take the time and effort to incorporate appropriate forms of technology into their teaching ought to be rewarded for their efforts. An example of how this could work may be drawn from my own university's considerations of diversity in evaluations of faculty teaching. At UCLA, faculty are encouraged to discuss their contributions in the area of diversity in their promotion and tenure materials—typically as part of their "Statement of Achievement." The same idea may be adopted relative to the use of technology in one's teaching.

Another area to consider is the importance of discipline-specific and interdisciplinary research on MOOC pedagogical and course-delivery practices. The idea here is that the MOOC course design and teaching strategies appropriate for a STEM course may not be the same as those best utilized in a social science or humanities course. Furthermore, particular MOOC strategies may be more helpful in the environment of interdisciplinary problem-based courses. Colleges and universities can help to advance knowledge about MOOC teaching and learning by supporting greater research and understanding into variations in courses and content for specific fields. A simple strategy might involve the allocation of a pool of funds for researching instructional practices and student learning outcomes relative to MOOCs. Additionally, to encourage a deeper application of social learning (and connectivist principles), such research funds could target the deployment of social media and online networking as strategies for promoting collaborative learning communities and collective intelligence.

A final consideration concerns the role faculty ought to play in ensuring high-quality online educational offerings, whether constructed in the format of the MOOC or through other course structures. It is the faculty, not the administration, ultimately charged with ensuring that courses are of high quality and that student learning is not compromised. Faculty organizations need to provide the necessary level of support and development for faculty involved in campus decision making about MOOCs. This should not be left to university administrators, who have different interests at stake. As a relatively new arena in education, MOOCs and other innovative forms of online education pose significant challenges for faculty members. Advancing knowledge about the complexities and variations of MOOC models and their role in supporting student learning is an important area faculty organizations ought to address.

The discussion in this section points to a variety of considerations for faculty members working at colleges and universities seeking to strengthen MOOC offerings. In light of the discussion, I offer the following summary points for better supporting faculty:

- Faculty need adequate IT support in order to strengthen their understanding and skills in the practice of Internet- and technology-based modes of course development and facilitation related to MOOCs. Support ought to include both group-based activities such as workshops and also more individualized approaches.
- Faculty involved in MOOCs should consider first and foremost the overall quality of the student learning experience. Although university administrators must conduct cost-benefit analyses as part of the broader university strategic mission, faculty members need to serve as the conscience of the university in terms of focusing on the quality of student learning. This may involve opposing efforts to adopt weaker versions of online education, such as the implementation of xMOOCs as replacements for face-to-face lower-division and remedial courses.
- Mechanisms need to be put into place that acknowledge and reward faculty for their efforts at incorporating and evaluating more advanced forms of technology as part of their teaching strategies, both in terms of MOOCs and more hybrid types of courses.

- Institutions should encourage faculty research on MOOCs across a range of disciplines and interdisciplinary fields. Based on existing evidence, it is reasonable to believe that academic subject area may have an impact on student engagement and learning in online environments (Xu and Jaggars 2014). Hence, the academic subject area of a MOOC should be considered as a key variable in empirical studies.
- In furthering faculty research on MOOCs, institutions may be well served when such programs link funding to best practices associated with online education, such as forms of teaching and learning grounded in the ideals of connectivism. Otherwise, institutions may perpetuate forms of online education counterproductive to deep student engagement and learning.

National- and State-Level Organizational Considerations

The fact that so many elite universities such as MIT, Harvard, Penn, Stanford, and Yale have contributed in significant ways to the advance of the MOOC is a huge factor in capturing the attention of national- and state-level entities, including the U.S. Department of Education, whose own data revealed that one in four U.S. college students enrolled in some type of online education in fall 2012. Given the growing momentum of MOOCs specifically and online education more broadly, there is an obvious need to examine policies across multiple sectors and levels of higher education.

One obvious example of how the online education landscape is altering policies and practices at the national level is evident in Moody's awarding a "credit positive" (essentially seeing a particular factor as a positive consideration in determining credit ratings) to the U.S. higher education industry on the strength of the willingness of postsecondary institutions to adapt technologies to the needs and interests of students. Moody's noted that "advancements in technology, online curriculum, and quality controls have made online education a more accepted and marketable tool for educational delivery" ("Colleges' Embrace" 2014).

At the federal level, there is good reason for key national agencies beyond the Department of Education to give more serious thought to the ways in which sensible MOOC policies might advance or undermine U.S. higher education and economic goals linked to meeting the changing needs of labor. For example, encouraging the proliferation of credential and degree programs based largely on xMOOCS may be detrimental to the U.S. national economy. On the one hand, simply using xMOOCs to further the credentialing of greater numbers of graduates may do little to actually upgrade marketable skills; such a strategy is likely to help foundations such as Lumina achieve its goal of increasing the percentage of U.S. citizens with degrees and credentials (described by Lumina as "Goal 2025"), but it may do little to elevate the quality and skills of the workforce. On the other hand, when national agencies invest resources into helping postsecondary institutions develop rich learning environments consistent with cMOOCs, they may actually further the skills, dispositions, and abilities increasingly necessary in fields defined by what Robert Reich (1992) once described as symbolic analysts. Such careers tend to require continuous knowledge and skill development; hence, exposing students to forms of online social learning rooted to some extent in collective intelligence is more likely to prepare them for the type of lifelong education they will need throughout their careers. If cMOOCs prove too expensive and cumbersome to support under particular conditions, then at the very least national agencies ought to encourage institutions to supplement xMOOCs with additional sources of academic support in the form of xsMOOCs. One specific strategy federal agencies could adopt, particularly those funding research and development such as the National Science Foundation and the National Institutes of Health, is to adopt funding programs aimed at developing more sophisticated social learning environments for subpopulations of MOOC users. This could go a long way toward moving xMOOCs more in the direction of cMOOCs and xsMOOCs.

Beyond the role of the federal government, key foundations such as Gates and Lumina could do a much better job of supporting the development of MOOCs stressing more connectivist-oriented principles, as opposed to giving so much attention to efficiency-minded outcomes and the automation of instructional materials. Although creating opportunities for more people to have the chance to pursue higher education credentials is a worthwhile goal, it is only significant when those credentials reflect meaningful and sustained educational engagement. Additionally, organizations such as the American Council on Education could play a key role in cultivating a more nuanced discussion of MOOCs and their role in higher education; for example, although its College Credit Recommendation Service (ACE CREDIT) is helpful in enabling nontraditional learners to access credentials, by the same token the program has been a tool in leveraging for-profits such as Coursera and their attempt to advance xMOOCs for educationally disadvantaged students. Greater differentiation in the assessment of MOOCs should be brought to bear on ACE's course evaluations, including the sort of epistemological, pedagogical, and hegemonic considerations raised as part of the discussion in this book.

State-level higher education commissions and agencies also must pay greater heed to the shortcomings identified by the MOOC research to this point. Accordingly, pushing public colleges and universities to further develop MOOCs or requiring such institutions to automatically accept MOOCs for credit, without recognizing the limitations of the xMOOC model, may be detrimental to broader statewide educational endeavors. The case of the California legislature's early fascination with MOOCs is instructive in that ultimately a good deal of time and energy was wasted on a knee-jerk reaction to the imagined cost savings of MOOCs.

Finally, the position of labor cannot be ignored as efforts move forward to strengthen the role of MOOCs at both national and state levels. The intellectual work of faculty in terms of the development of course materials and course-related content cannot simply be reproduced over and over again without adequate compensation. Organizations such as the American Association of University Professors and the National Education Association must take the lead in protecting faculty rights, along with state- and institutional-level faculty unions, senates, and associations. Exploitation of faculty labor as part of the democratization of knowledge—a central tenet of the OER, OCW, and MOOC movements—is the ultimate irony that at times is lost among the enthusiasm for MOOCs and their potential.

Concluding Thoughts

A central goal of this book is to bring a degree of balance to discussions involving the MOOC movement and what it may offer in terms of advancing higher education and higher learning. Having been seduced early on by the democratization-of-knowledge argument associated with the OCW movement more broadly and then MOOCs more specifically, I eventually had to adjust my thinking. I still believe MOOCs have a role to play in further democratizing knowledge, but my perspective is much more tempered. This was especially the case when I saw MOOCs increasingly being framed uncritically as solutions to the higher education access puzzle, although data and experience revealed shortcomings with the xMOOC model. MOOCs can and do contribute to expanding college access, but some of the MOOC experimentation has not gone well and warrants a degree of skepticism.

At the heart of my analysis in this book has been several critical questions embedded in much of the discussion: Do we really want superstar faculty from elite universities teaching masses of students at underfunded colleges and universities through the use of recorded lectures? Is a brick-and-mortar education to be reserved for the wealthiest of students while the rest are to be "MOOCed"? Are faculty at under-resourced institutions to be replaced by glorified teaching assistants offering support to thousands of students enrolled in xMOOCs? Do we truly want to further stratify our institutions of higher learning and in the process eliminate any hope of real social mobility? MOOCs as an educational reform movement have much to offer, but it is problematic to position MOOCs as a solution for the lack of willingness to support high-quality education for the least advantaged in our society. Although MOOCs are certainly innovative and can be great strategies for advancing learning in a variety of contexts, using them as replacement courses for face-to-face instruction at the least resourced colleges and universities is a practice that needs to be questioned.

Perhaps with adjustments, as in embracing some of the teaching and learning ideals associated with cMOOCs or adding elements of support as I suggest by the xsMOOC model, then possibilities may expand. I suspect that in the future we will see great experimentation with using hybrid xsMOOCs to benefit particular subpopulations, potentially stressing the advantages of social learning. There is already evidence coming from MRI findings to support this model.

To be fair to xMOOCs, teachers and informal learners around the world make use of this version of the MOOC for a variety of reasons, and the pattern of low completion rates is not really a good indicator of what they have to offer. As I have noted throughout this book, xMOOCs are an important vehicle for furthering the democratization of university courses and related knowledge. MOOCs have the potential to create opportunities for certain populations where little opportunity may have existed before. Although obviously we need to resist the proliferation of MOOC-based degree and certificate programs where engagement of students is minimal, this is not to suggest that successful degree programs cannot be built principally on the basis of MOOCs. I believe a good example is offered by the University of the People, which permits students to complete associate's and bachelor's degree programs in business administration and computer science by relying on MOOCs. For certain learners, completing a degree through UoPeople by piecing together MOOCs may work well, keeping in mind especially that not everyone learns in the same way and at the same pace. Providing such flexibility to self-motivated learners seems like a good idea. Here I must repeat the mantra of this book: MOOCs should be viewed as educational tools to be employed as part of a complex educational strategy, and in the case of UoPeople offerings, they seem to be used fittingly. Although MOOCs work well when used in this manner for a particular population of learners, we should not become victims of faulty logic and assume they achieve the same level of success when applied in other settings to different populations. Early MOOC research suggests that this is not the case.

In addition to the aforementioned concerns, I have identified other aspects of the MOOC movement that warrant serious attention. I have stressed the problem of a small group of elite providers dominating the MOOC landscape. This harms the democratization of knowledge. Also, I have pointed to the limited discussion and consideration of issues of diversity relative to the MOOC movement and to the OER and OCW movements as well. We cannot afford to lose sight of the fact that the world's social systems are rife with structural forms of inequality often linked to cultural differences and other forms of diversity. To ignore the reality that online learners—including MOOC users—have a diverse array of social identities, and that such identities matter, does not serve the interest of building challenging and cross-culturally enriching learning environs.

Additionally, I have devoted much attention to the MOOC movement and faculty work, both in terms of the potential deskilling of faculty labor among certain segments of the professorate and with regard to copyright and intellectual property issues. Seeking to advance educational opportunities for a range of learners in the form of MOOC initiatives should not come about by exploiting faculty labor. This is inconsistent with the sort of democratic values originally giving rise to OER, OCW, and MOOCs in the first place.

Finally, I see this book as offering a snapshot of a rather complex social movement during its early stage in development—a truly challenging endeavor. My view of MOOCs as a contribution to education, particularly higher education, contains elements of optimism as well as pessimism. I am mostly optimistic about the possibilities for MOOC experimentation to lead to new forms of teaching and learning likely to expand college access. Currently there is room for improvement, but I expect that in time higher education will see enhancements to the dominant xMOOC model in the form of xsMOOCs. I am less optimistic about MOOCs contributing to the kinds of empowering teaching and learning consistent with Freirian ideals. But even here my pessimism is tempered to a degree by possibilities presented by social learning, connectivism, and collective intelligence, all highlighted by the original cMOOC model. In time, I expect that the MOOC movement will be defined by its zealous high-tech experimentation in online education countenanced by a degree of skepticism about the role of technology in solving our most challenging educational problems.

Notes

CHAPTER 1: Introduction

1. See Dhawal Shah's "MOOCs in 2013: Breaking Down the Numbers" (December 22, 2013). www.edsurge.com/n/2013-12-22-moocs-in-2013-breaking-down-the-numbers.

2. In a previous work I employed the term "produsers" (or "prod-users") to capture this new Internet-based identity in which one assumes the role of user and producer simultaneously (see Rhoads, Berdan, and Toven-Lindsey 2013, 101).

3. See https://creativecommons.org/licenses/.

4. Although 2008 typically is the year linked to the recession, the *Wall Street Journal*, citing the National Bureau of Economic Research, reported that December 2007 actually marked the beginning of the recession, with the previous growth period having lasted seventy-three months, starting in November 2001 (Curran 2008).

5. See, for example, C. Allen (2011).

6. All one needs to do to confirm my analysis here is to visit Vedder's Center for College Affordability and Productivity website and review some of his blog posts about the wasted research in the social sciences and humanities: http://centerforcollegeaffordability .org/. The only real research is apparently that which promotes economic development, while anything serving to advance social, cultural, or historical concerns is irrelevant.

7. Although the Siemens and Downes course is often identified as the first MOOC, it is important to recognize that other educationalists, mostly working out of Canada, had been experimenting with innovative online formats for years. In this sense, the Siemens and Downes course may be understood as the outcome of many minds operating in a manner akin to the collective intelligence stressed by the MOOC movement (especially in terms of cMOOCs).

8. The term "MOOC," or "massive open online course," is believed to have emerged from a Skype conversation between Dave Cormier and George Siemens about what to actually call the CCK08 course constructed by Siemens and Stephen Downes. Cormier (2008) reportedly suggested the idea of "massive open online course." Obviously, the name stuck.

CHAPTER 2: The Organizational System of the World of the MOOC

1. Here I believe it is safe to assume that today much of distance education is conducted online.

2. Some of the thinking presented in this section grew from collaboration with my doctoral students, namely Jennifer Berdan Lozano, Sayil Camacho, and Brit Toven-Lindsey.

3. The authors of this study note a very low response rate: 8.5 percent of students who had completed at least one assignment and 4.3 percent from all students who had enrolled in a course (including those who did not return to any course webpage after enrolling). It is not clear, though, how nonrespondent bias might have influenced the findings.

4. See http://collegeopentextbooks.ning.com/profiles/blogs/open-doors-group-is -seeking-volunteer-staff-for-its-upcoming-mooc.

5. There is no agreement on the point that "open" in "massive open online courses" means free. Some see "open" as simply implying that anyone can enroll in a course, even if a fee is charged, while others suggest that the MOOC's "openness" is constituted by inviting a wide array of learners into the educational experience. For example, Jesse Stommel (2012) in an essay titled, "The March of the MOOCs: Monstrous Open Online Courses," argued that "open" is "dangerously misread. The pedagogical value in openness is that it helps create dialogue by increasing access and bringing at once disparate learning spaces into conversation. Open, though, does not mean free. Everything is monetized, whether overtly, indirectly, or insidiously." I respect Stommel's point that costs are incurred in constructing a MOOC but nonetheless prefer to stress the importance of the fee-less quality of most MOOCs, in part because I emphasize the democratic potential of MOOCs to expand access and engagement with knowledge (in other words, the cost is not covered by the user or learner). For me, charging a fee as part of offering a MOOC closes the door to a particular segment of the population and hardly constitutes openness.

6. See http://robots. stanford.edu/.

7. See www.coursera.org/about/.

8. See http://blog.coursera.org/post/40080531667/signaturetrack.

9. See www.acenet.edu/news-room/Pages/College-Credit-Recommendation-Service -CREDIT.aspx.

10. See www.moocresearch.com/mooc-research-initiative-grants-awarded.

11. See http://open.media.mit.edu/about-us/.

12. See www.ocwconsortium.org/about-ocw/.

13. See http://oerconsortium.org/.

14. See http://blog.coursera.org/post/63406806112/a-new-partnership-to-bring-cour sera-to-the-hundreds-of.

CHAPTER 3: Connectivism, Social Learning, and the cMOOC/xMOOC Distinction

1. Downes discussed this briefly on his personal Google+webpage: https://plus.google .com/109526159908242471749/posts/LEwaKxL2MaM.

2. As I note in chapter 2, not everyone agrees that MOOCs must be free. See Jesse Stommel (2012) for another take on the meaning of "open" relative to MOOCs.

3. The idea of the "cost disease" (also known as the "Baumol effect") and the challenges of higher education cost containment is connected to an earlier argument advanced by William J. Baumol and William G. Bowen (1966) in their book *Performing Arts—The Economic Dilemma: A Study of Problems Common to Theater, Opera, Music, and Dance.* The essential idea is that there are elements to the performing arts that interrupt the typical economic principle that salary (or wage) increases are tied to improved labor productivity.

4. The findings highlighted here (UC Irvine and UW) derive from studies not yet published at the time of the writing of this book, but the preliminary, non–peer reviewed summaries were posted as part of the MRI website research reports at www.moocresearch .com/reports. Other results of MRI studies, such as projects led by Rebecca Eynon, Laura Perna, and Allison Littlejohn, among others, are discussed at different points in this book.

CHAPTER 4: Blowback and Resistance to the MOOC Movement

1. My discussion of the five key problems in this chapter builds on and extends a paper previously published with two of my doctoral students (Rhoads, Berdan, and Toven-Lindsey 2013).

2. The five problems delineated in this chapter help to address several of my key theses. The problem of epistemology and the problem of pedagogy concern thesis 4 and shortcomings associated with xMOOCs. The problem of hegemony is linked to thesis 5 and the problematic role of elite universities. The problem of diversity addresses thesis 6 and the absence of serious diversity dialogue within the MOOC movement. Finally, the problem of faculty labor is tied to thesis 7 and the implications MOOCs have for faculty work.

3. A caveat must be offered here: The findings of the Perna group and others as well were based on early renditions of the MOOC, of xMOOCs in particular. In time, active engagement on the part of course enrollees may increase as insights are gleaned over the years. I fully expect this to be the case, but some shortcomings may be more difficult to overcome than others.

4. A summary of this study is available at Allison Littlejohn's website, "Little by Little-john": http://littlebylittlejohn.com/professional-learning-in-moocs/. Also, there is a methodological discussion of the project by Colin Milligan, Allison Littlejohn, and Obiageli Ukadike titled "Professional Learning in Massive Open Online Courses," but it seems to pre-date their actual findings.

5. These findings are also part of the MOOC Research Initiative in a study led by Littlejohn with Milligan (2014).

6. The Xu and Jaggars (2014) study was based on results from over forty thousand community and technical college students in the state of Washington.

CHAPTER 5: Conclusion

1. This research was discussed in chapter 3, and a preliminary report is offered at the Gates-funded MOOC Research Initiative website: www.moocresearch.com/wp-content/uploads/2014/06/C9142_Warschauer_MOOC_Research_Initiative9142-pub-version.pdf.

Bibliography

AAUP. 2013. "Defending the Freedom to Innovate: Faculty Intellectual Property Rights after Stanford v. Roche." Report from the American Association of University Professors. www.aaup.org/report.

Adelman, Chad, and Kevin Carey. 2009. "Ready to Assemble: Grading State Higher Education Accountability Systems." Research report from Education Sector, Washington, DC.

Allen, Charlotte. 2011. "How Productive Do Professors Have to Be?" Center for the American University, Manhattan Institute (24 July). www.mindingthecampus.com.

Allen, I. Elaine, and Jeff Seaman. 2007. *Online Nation: Five Years of Growth in Online Learning.* Needham, MA: Sloan Consortium.

Alliance for Higher Education and Democracy (AHEAD). 2014. "What's AHEAD: Key Trends in Higher Education (Poll #1: Massive Open Online Courses)." Report from the University of Pennsylvania's AHEAD (April). www.gse.upenn.edu/pdf/ahead/whats_ahead/01_oocs.pdf.

Anderson, Nick. 2013. "MOOCs—Here Come the Credentials." *Washington Post* (9 January). www.washingtonpost.com.

Apple, Michael W. 2000. "Between Neoliberalism and Neoconservatism: Education and Conservatism in a Global Context." In *Globalization and Education: Critical Perspectives,* edited by Nicholas C. Burbules and Carlos Alberto Torres, 57–77. New York: Routledge.

Arbaugh, J. B., and Raquel Benbunan-Fich. 2006. "An Investigation of Epistemological and Social Dimensions of Teaching in Online Learning Environments." *Academy of Management Learning and Education* 5(4): 435–447.

Aronowitz, Stanley. 2000. *The Knowledge Factory: Dismantling the Corporate University and Creating True Higher Learning.* Boston: Beacon Press.

Astin, Alexander W. 1993. *What Matters in College? Four Critical Years Revisited.* San Francisco: Jossey-Bass.

———. 1999. "How the Liberal Arts College Affects Students. *Daedalus* 128(1): 77–100.

———. 2014. "To MOOC or Not to MOOC the Liberal Arts? Why Not Consult the Evidence?" Keynote address at MOOCing the Liberal Arts? Technology and Relationship in Liberal Arts Education, The Thirteenth Annual Conversation on the Liberal Arts, Gaede Institute for the Liberal Arts, Santa Barbara, California, 15 February.

Atkins, Daniel E., John Seely Brown, and Allen L. Hammond. 2007. "A Review of the Open Educational Resources (OER) Movement: Achievements, Challenges, and New Opportunities." San Francisco: Creative Commons License.

"Attack of the MOOCs, The." 2013. *The Economist* (20 July). www.economist.com.

Banks, James A. 2010. "Multicultural Education: Characteristics and Goals." In *Multicultural Education: Issues and Perspectives* (7th ed.), edited by James A. Banks and Cherry A. McGee Banks, 3–32. Hoboken, NJ: John Wiley & Sons.

Barabasi, Albert-Laszlo. 2003. *Linked: How Everything Is Connected to Everything Else and What It Means for Business, Science, and Everyday Life.* New York: Plume Books.

Baraniuk, Richard G. 2008. "Challenges and Opportunities for the Open Education Movement: A Connexions Case Study." In *Opening Up Education: The Collective Advancement of Education through Open Technology, Open Content, and Open Knowledge* (Creative Commons edition), edited by Toru Iiyoshi and M. S. Vijay Kumar, 229–246. Princeton, NJ: Carnegie Foundation for the Advancement of Teaching; Cambridge, MA: MIT Press.

Bauerlein, Mark. 2011. "Faculty Productivity Is Coming." *Chronicle of Higher Education* (29 July). http://chronicle.com.

Baumol, William J., and William G. Bowen. 1966. *Performing Arts—the Economic Dilemma: A Study of Problems Common to Theater, Opera, Music, and Dance.* New York: Twentieth Century Fund.

Becker, Gary S. 2013. "The Worldwide Boom in Higher Education." Invited talk at the Institute of Governmental Studies, University of California, Berkeley, 20 March.

Biglan, Anthony. 1973a. "The Characteristics of Subject Matter in Different Academic Areas." *Journal of Applied Psychology* 57(3): 195–203.

———. 1973b. "Relationships between Subject Matter Characteristics and the Structure and Output of University Departments." *Journal of Applied Psychology* 57(3): 204–213.

"Big Three, at a Glance, The." 2012. *New York Times* (2 November). www.nytimes.com.

Bissell, Ahrash N. 2009. "Permission Granted: Open Licensing for Educational Resources." *Open Learning: The Journal of Open, Distance, and e-Learning* 24(1): 97–106.

Blumer, Herbert. 1990. *Industrialization as an Agent of Social Change: A Critical Analysis.* Hawthorne, NY: Aldine.

Board of Governors, State University System of Florida. 2013. "Task Force on Postsecondary Online Education in Florida Final Report" (9 December).

Bok, Derek. 2003. *Universities in the Marketplace: The Commercialization of Higher Education.* Princeton, NJ: Princeton University Press.

Bonk, Curtis J. 2009. *The World Is Open: How Web Technology Is Revolutionizing Education.* San Francisco: Jossey-Bass.

Bowen, William G. 2013. *Higher Education in the Digital Age.* Princeton, NJ: Princeton University Press.

Braverman, Harry. 1974. *Labor and Monopoly Capital: The Degradation of Work in the Twentieth Century.* New York: Monthly Review Press.

Breslow, Lori, David E. Pritchard, Jennifer DeBoer, Glenda S. Stump, Andrew D. Ho, and Daniel T. Seaton. 2013. "Studying Learning in the Worldwide Classroom: Research into edX's First MOOC." *Research and Practice in Assessment* 8: 13–25.

Brown, John Seely. 2008. "Foreword: Creating a Culture of Learning." *Opening Up Education: The Collective Advancement of Education through Open Technology, Open Content, and Open Knowledge* (Creative Commons edition), edited by Toru Iiyoshi and M. S. Vijay Kumar, xi–xvii. Princeton, NJ: Carnegie Foundation for the Advancement of Teaching and Cambridge, MA: MIT Press.

Brown, John Seely, and Richard Adler. 2008. "Minds on Fire: Open Education, the Long Tail, and Learning 2.0." *EDUCAUSE Review* 43(1): 16–32.

California Senate. 2013. "SB-520 Student Instruction: California Online Student Incentive Grant Programs." California Legislative Information. http://leginfo.legislature.ca.gov/faces/billNavClient.xhtml?bill_id=201320140SB520.

Carey, Kevin. 2012. "Into the Future with MOOCs." *Chronicle of Higher Education* (3 September). http://chronicle.com.

Carson, Steve. 2009. "The Unwalled Garden: Growth of the OpenCourseWare Consortium, 2001–2008." *Open Learning* 24(1): 23–29.

Cervinschi, Cezar Liviu, and Diana Butucea. 2010. "Integration of Web Technologies in Software Applications. Is Web 2.0 a Solution?" *Database Systems Journal* 1(2), 39–44.

Christensen, Gayle, Andrew Steinmetz, Brandon Alcorn, Amy Bennett, Deirdre Woods, and Ezekiel J. Emanuel. 2013. "The MOOC Phenomenon: Who Takes Massive Open Online Courses and Why?" Unpublished research paper (6 November). http://papers.ssrn.com/sol3/papers.cfm?abstract_id=2350964.

Chronicle Staff. 2014. "Higher-Ed Leaders Worry Most about Declining Enrollment, Survey Finds." *Chronicle of Higher Education* (17 September). http://chronicle.com/blogs.

"Colleges' Embrace of Online Learning Is a 'Credit Positive.'" 2014. *Chronicle of Higher Education* (13 June). http://chronicle.com/blogs.

Comer, Denise, and Dorian Canelas. 2014. "Writing to Learn and Learning to Write across the Disciplines." Research report from the MOOC Research Institute. www.moocresearch.com.

Cormier, Dave. 2008. "The CCK08 MOOC—Connectivism Course, 1/4 Way." *Dave's Educational Blog* (2 October). http://davecormier.com/edblog/2008/10/02/the-cck08-mooc-connectivism-course-14-way.

Cormier, Dave, and George Siemens. 2010. "Through the Open Door: Open Courses as Research, Learning, and Engagement." *EDUCAUSE Review* 45(4): 30–39.

Cormode, Graham, and Balachander Krishnamurthy. 2008. "Key Differences between Web 1.0 and 2.0." *First Monday* 13(6). http://journals.uic.edu/ojs/index.php/fm/article/view/2125/1972#author.

Council of Presidents of Arizona's Board of Regents. 2010. "The Arizona Higher Education Enterprise: Strategic Realignment 2010 Forward." (September). http://azregents.asu.edu/UAPresSearchDocs/Enterprise%20Plan%20-%20The%20Arizona%20Higher%20Education%20Enterprise.pdf.

Couros, Alec. 2008. "Safety and Social Networking: How Can We Maximize the Learning Power of the Participatory Websites while Ensuring Students Are Protected and Behave Responsibly?" *Technology & Learning* 28(7): 20–22.

———. 2009. "Open, Connected, Social—Implications for Educational Design." *Campus-Wide Information Systems* 26(3): 232–239.

Crenshaw, Kimberle. 1991. "Mapping the Margins: Intersectionality, Identity Politics, and Violence against Women of Color." *Stanford Law Review* 43(6): 1241–1299.

Curran, Rob. 2008. "U.S. Entered a Recession a Year Ago, NBER Says." *Wall Street Journal* (1 December). http://online.wsj.com.

Davidson, Cathy N. 2013. "Clearing Up Some Myths about MOOCs." HASTAC (Humanities, Arts, Science, and Technology Alliance and Collaboratory) (11 June). www.hastac.org.

———. 2014a. "10 Things I've Learned (So Far) from Making a Meta-MOOC." *Hybrid Pedagogy* (16 January). www.hybridpedagogy.com.

———. 2014b. "Why Higher Education Demands a Paradigm Shift." *Public Culture* 26(1) (Issue 72): 3–11.

Dearen, Jason. 2013. "San Jose State Suspends Online Courses." *San Jose Mercury News* (17 July). www.mercurynews.com/news.

DeBoer, Jennifer, Andrew D. Ho, Glenda S. Stump, and Lori Breslow. 2014. "Changing 'Course': Reconceptualizing Educational Variables for Massive Open Online Courses." *Educational Researcher* 43(2): 74–84.

DeSantis, Nick. 2012. "Stanford Professor Gives Up Teaching Position, Hopes to Reach 500,000 Students at Online Start-Up." *Chronicle of Higher Education* (23 January). http://chronicle.com.

DiNucci, Darcy. 1999. "Fragmented Future." *Print* 53(4): 32, 221–222.

DiSalvio, Philip. 2013. "New Directions for Higher Education: Q&A with Lumina's Merisotis on Increasing College Enrollment and Graduation." *New England Journal of Higher Education* (17 June). www.nebhe.org.

Downes, Stephen. 2007. "Models for Sustainable Open Educational Resources." *Interdisciplinary Journal of Knowledge and Learning Objects* 3: 29–44.

———. 2011. "Connectivism and Connective Knowledge." *Huffington Post* (5 January). www.huffingtonpost.com.

———. 2013. "Assessment in MOOCs." *Half an Hour* (4 May). http://halfanhour.blogspot.com/2013/05/assessment-in-moocs.html

Edinburgh University. 2013. "MOOCs @ Edinburgh 2013—Report #1." (10 May).

EDUCAUSE. 2012. "What Campus Leaders Need to Know about MOOCs." Executive Briefing. www.educause.edu.

Else, Holly. 2014. "Brazil's Home-Grown MOOC, Verduca, Has High Hopes." *Times Higher Education* (14 January). www.timeshighereducation.co.uk.

Engberg, Mark E., and Sylvia S. Hurtado. 2011. "Developing Pluralistic Skills and Dispositions in College: Examining Racial/Ethnic Group Differences." *Journal of Higher Education* 82(4): 416–443.

Eynon, Rebecca. 2014. "Conceptualising Interaction and Learning in MOOC." Research report from the MOOC Research Institute. www.moocresearch.com.

Foucault, Michel. 1972. *The Archaeology of Knowledge*. Translated by A. M. Sheridan Smith. New York: Pantheon Books.

———. 1978. *The History of Sexuality Volume 1: An Introduction*. New York: Random House.

———. 1979. *Discipline and Punish*. Translated by Alan Sheridan. New York: Vintage Books.

———. 1980. *Power/Knowledge: Selected Interviews and Other Writings, 1972–1977*. Edited by Colin Gordan. New York: Pantheon.

Fowler, Geoffrey A. 2013. "An Early Report Card on Massive Open Online Courses." *Wall Street Journal* (8 October). http://online.wsj.com.

Freire, Paulo. 1970. *Pedagogy of the Oppressed*. Translated by Myra Bergman Ramos. New York: Continuum.

Friedman, Thomas L. 2005. *The World Is Flat: A Brief History of the 21st Century*. New York: Farrar, Straus and Giroux.

———. 2011. "Justice Goes Global." *New York Times* (14 June). www.nytimes.com.

———. 2013. "Revolution Hits the Universities." *New York Times* (26 February). www.nytimes.com.

Gates, Bill. 2010. "Annual Letter 2010." Bill & Melinda Gates Foundation. www.gatesfoundation.org.

Gilbert, Daniel A. 2013. "The Generation of Public Intellectuals: Corporate Universities, Graduate Employees and the Academic Labor Movement." *Labor Studies Journal* 38(1): 32–46.

Giroux, Henry A. 1988. *Teachers as Intellectuals: Towards a Critical Pedagogy of Learning*. Westport, CT: Bergin & Garvey.

———. 1990. "Curriculum Theory, Textual Authority, and the Role of Teachers as Public Intellectuals." *Journal of Curriculum and Supervision* 5(4): 361–383.

———. 2002. "Neoliberalism, Corporate Culture, and the Promise of Higher Education: The University as a Democratic Public Sphere." *Harvard Educational Review* 72(4): 425–464.

Grainger, Barney. 2013. "Massive Open Online Course (MOOC) Report 2013." University of London International Academy.

Granovetter, Mark S. 1973. "The Strength of Weak Ties." *American Journal of Sociology* 78(6): 1360–1380.

———. 1983. "The Strength of Weak Ties: A Network Theory Revisited." *Sociological Theory* 1: 201–233.

Haber, Jonathan. 2014. *MOOCs*. Cambridge, MA: MIT Press.

Hardin, Garrett. 1968. "The Tragedy of the Commons." *Science* 162: 1243–1248.

Hess, Charlotte, and Elinor Ostrom, eds. 2007. *Understanding Knowledge as a Commons: From Theory to Practice.* Cambridge, MA: MIT Press.

Hewlett Foundation. 2013. "Open Educational Resources: Breaking the Lockbox on Education." White Paper from the William and Flora Hewlett Foundation, November.

Holzl, Alan. 1999. "Designing for Diversity within Online Learning Environments." In QUT, Brisbane, Queensland, Australia for the Annual Australasian Society for Computers in Learning in Tertiary Education (ASCILITE 99) Conference, December. www.ascilite.org.au/conferences/brisbane99/papers/holzl.pdf.

hooks, bell. 1994. *Teaching to Transgress: Education as the Practice of Freedom.* New York: Routledge.

Howard, Jennifer. 2014. "New Alliance Aims to Answer Authors' Questions about Rights." *Chronicle of Higher Education* (21 May). http://chronicle.com/article.

Howard, Tyrone C. 2003. "Culturally Relevant Pedagogy: Ingredients for Critical Teacher Reflection." *Theory into Practice* 42(3): 195–202.

Huijser, Henk, Tas Bedford, and David Bull. 2008. "OpenCourseWare, Global Access, and the Right to Education: Real Access or Marketing Ploy?" *International Review of Research in Open and Distance Learning* 9(1). www.irrodl.org/index.php/irrodl/article/view/446/1002.

Irvine, Valerie. 2009. "The Emergence of Choice in 'Multi-Access' Learning Environments: Transferring Locus of Control of Course Access to the Learner." In Proceedings of World Conference on Educational Multimedia, Hypermedia and Telecommunications 2009, edited by George Siemens and Catherine Fulford, 746–752. Chesapeake, VA: Association for the Advancement of Computing in Education.

Irvine, Valerie, Jillianne Code, and Luke Richards. 2013. "Realigning Higher Education for the 21st-Century Learner through Multi-Access Learning." *MERLOT Journal of Online Learning and Teaching* 9(2).

Jaschik, Scott. 2013. "Harvard Profs Push Back." *Inside Higher Ed* (28 May). www.insidehighered.com.

Johnson, Ben, and Tom McCarthy. 2000. "Casual Labor and the Future of the Academy." *Thought & Action* (Summer): 107–120.

Kamenetz, Anya. 2013. "Open University: Coursera Partners with 10 Major State Schools." *Fast Company* (30 May). www.fastcompany.com

Kapitzke, Cushla. 2000. "Information Technology as Cultural Capital: Shifting the Boundaries of Power." *Education and Information Technologies* 5(1): 49–62.

Keeley-Browne, Elizabeth. 2011. *Cyber-Ethnography: The Emerging Research Approach for 21st Century Research Investigation.* Hershey, PA: IGI Global.

Kenney, Martin, ed. 2000. *Understanding Silicon Valley: The Anatomy of an Entrepreneurial Region*. Stanford, CA: Stanford University Press.

Kingkade, Tyler. 2012. "For-Profit Colleges Collect $32 Billion, 3 Lose Federal Aid Eligibility for Failing 90/10 Rule." *Huffington Post* (28 September). www.huffingtonpost .com.

Koenig, Rebecca. 2014. "Optimism about MOOCs Fades in Campus IT Offices." *Chronicle of Higher Education* (1 October). http://chronicle.com.

Kolowich, Steve. 2013a. "Coursera Takes a Nuanced View of Course Dropout Rates." *Chronicle of Higher Education* (8 April). http://chronicle.com.

———. 2013b. "The Minds behind the MOOCs: The Professors Who Make the MOOCs." *Chronicle of Higher Education* (18 March). http://chronicle.com.

———. 2014a. "Coursera Chief: Reach of Teaching Will Define Great Universities." *Chronicle of Higher Education* (19 June). http://chronicle.com.

———. 2014b. "Coursera Hires Former Yale President as Its Chief Executive." *Chronicle of Higher Education* (24 March). http://chronicle.com.

———. 2014c. "George Siemens Gets Connected." *Chronicle of Higher Education* (13 January). http://chronicle.com.

———. 2014d. "New U. of California President Plays Down Online Education." *Chronicle of Higher Education* (27 March). http://chronicle.com.

———. 2014e. "2014: The Year the Media Stopped Caring about MOOCs?" *Chronicle of Higher Education* (14 April). http://chronicle.com.

Kop, Rita. 2011. "The Challenges to Connectivist Learning on Open Online Networks: Learning Experiences during a Massive Open Online Course." *The International Review of Research in Open and Online Learning* 12(3), 19–38.

Kop, Rita, Helene Fournier, and John Sui Fai Mak. 2011. "A Pedagogy of Abundance or a Pedagogy to Support Human Beings: Participant Support on Massive Open Online Courses." *The International Review of Research in Open and Distance Learning* 12(7): 74–93.

Korn, Melissa. 2013. "Online Education Startup Coursera Raises $43 Million." *Wall Street Journal* (10 July). http://blogs.wsj.com.

Kozinets, Robert V. 2010. *Netnography: Doing Ethnographic Research Online*. London: Sage.

Ladson-Billings, G. 1995. "Toward a Theory of Culturally Relevant Pedagogy." *American Educational Research Journal* 32(3): 465–491.

Landler, Mark. 2008. "U.S. Housing Collapse Spreads Overseas." *New York Times* (13 April). www.nytimes.com.

Lauzon, Allan C. 1999. "Situating Cognition and Crossing Borders: Resisting the Hegemony of Mediated Education." *British Journal of Educational Technology* 30(3): 261–276.

———. 2000. Distance Education and Diversity: Are They Compatible? *American Journal of Distance Education* 14(2): 61–70.

Leckart, Steven. 2012. "The Stanford Education Experiment Could Change Higher Learning Forever." *Wired* (20 March). www.wired.com.

Lewin, Tamar. 2012a. "Colorado State to Offer Credits for Online Class." *New York Times* (6 September). www.nytimes.com.

———. 2012b. "Instruction for Masses Knocks Down Campus Walls." *New York Times* (4 March). www.nytimes.com.

———. 2013. "Universities Abroad Join Partnerships on the Web." *New York Times* (20 February). www.nytimes.com.

Littlejohn, Allison, and Colin Milligan 2014. "Professional Learning through Massive Open Online Courses." Research report from the MOOC Research Institute. www .moocresearch.com.

Losh, Elizabeth. 2014. *The War on Learning: Gaining Ground in the Digital University.* Cambridge, MA: MIT Press.

Lye, Colleen, and James Vernon. 2014. "The Erosion of Faculty Rights." *Chronicle of Higher Education* (19 May). http://chronicle.com.

Lyotard, Jean-François. 1984. *The Postmodern Condition.* Minneapolis: University of Minnesota Press.

Lytle, Ryan. 2011. "Study: Online Education Continues Growth." *U.S. News & World Report* (11 November). www.usnews.com.

MacLeod, Jay. 1995. *Ain't No Makin' It: Aspirations and Attainment in a Low-Income Neighborhood.* Boulder, CO: Westview Press.

"Major Players in the MOOC Universe." 2013. *Chronicle of Higher Education* (29 April). http://chronicle.com.

Maldonado, David E. Z., Robert A. Rhoads, and Tracy Lachica Buenavista. 2005. "The Student-Initiated Retention Project: Theoretical Contributions and the Role of Self-Empowerment." *American Educational Research Journal* 42(4): 605–638.

Mangan, Katherine. 2010. "Texas A&M's Bottom-Line Ratings of Professors Find That Most Are Cost-Effective." *Chronicle of Higher Education* (15 September). https://chronicle.com.

———. 2011. "U. of Texas Adopts Plan to Publish Performance Data on Professors and Campuses." *Chronicle of Higher Education* (25 August). https://chronicle.com.

———. 2013. "MOOCs Could Help 2-Year Colleges and Their Students, Says Bill Gates." *Chronicle of Higher Education* (3 October). http://chronicle.com.

McDonough, Patricia M. 1997. *Choosing College: How Social Class and Schools Structure Opportunity.* Albany: SUNY Press.

Mirrlees, Tanner, and Shahid Alvi. 2014. "Taylorizing Academia, Deskilling Professors and Automating Higher Education: The Recent Role of MOOCs." *Journal for Critical Education Policy Studies* 12(2). www.jceps.com.

Morris, Sean Michael, and Jesse Stommel. 2012. "A MOOC Is Not a Thing: Emergence, Disruption, and Higher Education." *Hybrid Pedagogy* (19 November). www.hybrid pedagogy.com.

———. 2014. "Is It Okay to Be a Luddite?" *Hybrid Pedagogy* (17 June). www.hybridpeda gogy.com.

Nesterko, Sergiy O., Svetlana Dotsenko, Qiuyi Hu, Daniel Seaton, Justin Reich, Isaac Chuang, and Andrew Ho. 2014. "Evaluating Geographic Data in MOOCs." *Neural Information Processing Systems.*

Newall, Mallory. 2009. "Higher Education Budget Cuts: How Are They Affecting Students?" Report 09-27 from the California Postsecondary Education Commission, Sacramento, CA.

Newman, Jonah. 2014. "Almost One-Third of All Foreign Students in U.S. Are from China." *Chronicle of Higher Education* (7 February). http://chronicle.com/blogs.

Noble, David F. 2001. *Digital Diploma Mills: The Automation of Higher Education.* New York: Monthly Review Press.

Norris, Pippa. 2001. *Digital Divide: Civic Engagement, Information Poverty, and the Internet Worldwide.* Cambridge: Cambridge University Press.

OECD. 2007. *Giving Knowledge for Free: The Emergence of Open Educational Resources.* Paris: Center for Educational Research and Innovation, Organisation for Economic Co-operation and Development.

O'Neil, Megan. 2013. "Obama Proposals for Colleges Highlight Online Courses." *Chronicle of Higher Education* (22 August). http://chronicle.com.

O'Reilly, Tim. 2006. "What Is Web 2.0?" http://oreilly.com/web2/archive/what-is-web-20.html.

O'Reilly, Tim, and John Battelle. 2009. "Web Squared: Web 2.0 Five Years On." Special Report, Web 2.0 Summit. www.web2summit.com/web2009/public/schedule/detail/10194.

Pappano, Laura. 2012. "The Year of the MOOC." *New York Times* (2 November). www.nytimes.com.

Parry, Marc. 2010. "Online, Bigger Classes May Be Better Classes." *Chronicle of Higher Education* (29 August). http://chronicle.com.

Perelman, Les. 2014. "Flunk the Robo-Graders." *Boston Globe* (30 April). www.bostonglobe.com.

Perez-Hernandez, Danya. 2014. "Coursera Seeks to Create a 'Global Translator Community.'" *Chronicle of Higher Education* (29 April). http://chronicle.com.

Perna, Laura, Alan Ruby, Robert Boruch, Nicole Wang, Janie Scull, Chad Evans, and Seher Amad. 2013. "The Life Cycle of a Million MOOC Users." Paper presented at the MOOC Research Initiative Conference, Austin, Texas, December.

Petriglieri, Gianpiero. 2013. "Let Them Eat MOOCs." *Harvard Business Review* Blog Network (9 October). http://blogs.hbr.org/2013/10/let-them-eat-moocs/.

Piech, Chris, Jonathan Huang, Zhenghao Chen, Chuong Do, Andrew Ng, and Daphne Koller. 2013. "Tuned Models of Peer Assessment in MOOCs." http://arxiv.org/abs/1307.2579.

Poellhuber, Bruno, Normand Roy, Ibtihel Bouchoucha, and Terry Anderson. 2014. "The Relationships between the Motivational Profiles and Persistence of MOOC Participants." Research report from the MOOC Research Institute. www.moocresearch.com.

President's Council of Advisors on Science and Technology (PCAST). 2013. "Letter to President Obama." Executive Office of the President, December, Washington, DC.

Press, Andrea, and Francesca Tripodi. 2014. "The New Misogyny." *Chronicle of Higher Education* (2 July). http://chronicle.com/blogs.

Rees, Jonathan. 2013. "Peer Grading Can't Work." *Inside Higher Ed* (5 March). www.insidehighered.com.

———. 2014. "The Taylorization of the Historian's Workplace." *Perspectives on History* (February). www.historians.org/publications-and-directories/perspectives-on-history.

Reich, Robert B. 1992. *The Work of Nations: Preparing Ourselves for 21st-Century Capitalism.* New York: Vintage Books.

Rhoads, Robert A. 1998. *Freedom's Web: Student Activism in an Age of Cultural Diversity.* Baltimore: Johns Hopkins University Press.

———. 2003. "Globalization and Resistance in the United States and Mexico: The Global Potemkin Village." *Higher Education* 45(2): 223–250.

———. 2013. "The Open Courseware Movement and MOOC Madness: Exploring Democratic and Anti-Democratic Potentialities." Invited presentation at UCLA's Uncommon Conversations Colloquium Series, Los Angeles, June.

Rhoads, Robert A., Jennifer Berdan, and Brit Toven-Lindsey. 2013. "The Open Courseware Movement in Higher Education: Unmasking Power and Raising Questions about the Movement's Democratic Potential." *Educational Theory* 63(1): 87–109.

Rhoads, Robert A., Shuai Li, and Lauren Ilano. 2015. "The Global Quest to Build World-Class Universities: Toward a Social Justice Agenda." In *Global Competition in Higher Education* (New Directions in Higher Education), edited by Laura M. Portnoi and Sylvia S. Bagley. San Francisco: Jossey-Bass.

Rhoads, Robert A., and Amy Liu. 2009. "Globalization, Social Movements, and the American University: Implications for Research and Practice." *Higher Education: Handbook of Theory and Practice* 24: 277–320.

Rhoads, Robert A., and Liliana Mina. 2001. "The Student Strike at the National Autonomous University of Mexico: A Political Analysis." *Comparative Education Review* 45(3): 334–353.

Rhoads, Robert A., and Gary Rhoades. 2005. "Graduate Employee Unionization as Symbol of and Challenge to the Corporatization of U.S. Research Universities." *Journal of Higher Education* 76(3): 243–275.

Rhoads, Robert A., and Katalin Szelényi. 2011. *Global Citizenship and the University: Advancing Social Life and Relations in an Interdependent World*. Stanford, CA: Stanford University Press.

Rivard, Ry. 2013a. "Measuring the MOOC Dropout Rate." *Inside Higher Ed* (8 March). www.insidehighered.com.

———. 2013b. "Udacity Project on 'Pause.'" *Inside Higher Ed* (18 July). www.insidehighered.com.

———. 2013c. "The World Is Not Flat." *Inside Higher Ed* (25 April). www.insidehighered.com.

Rodriguez, C. Osvaldo. 2012. "MOOCs and the AI-Stanford Like Courses: Two Successful and Distinct Course Formats for Massive Open Online Courses." *European Journal of Open, Distance and E-Learning*. http://files.eric.ed.gov/fulltext/EJ982976.pdf.

———. 2013. "The Concept of Openness Behind C and X-MOOCs (Massive Open Online Courses)." *Open Praxis* 5(1): 67–73.

Rose, Mike. 2014. *Why School? Reclaiming Education for All of Us* (2nd ed.). New York: New Press.

Said, Edward W. 1993. *Culture and Imperialism*. New York: Vintage Books.

Saxenian, AnnaLee. 1996. *Regional Advantage: Culture and Competition in Silicon Valley and Route 128*. Cambridge, MA: Harvard University Press.

Schmidt, Peter. 2013. "AAUP Sees MOOCs as Spawning New Threats to Professors' Intellectual Property." *Chronicle of Higher Education* (12 June). http://chronicle.com.

Schuman, Rebecca. 2013. "The King of MOOCs Abdicates the Throne: Sebastian Thrun and Udacity's 'Pivot' toward Corporate Training." *Slate* (19 November). www.slate.com.

Scott, John. C. 1999. "The Chautauqua Movement: Revolution in Popular Higher Education." *Journal of Higher Education* 70(4): 389–412.

Selingo, Jeffrey. 2012. "Did Anyone Ask the Students? Part I." *Chronicle of Higher Education* (1 May). http://chronicle.com/blogs.

———. 2013. "Attitudes in Innovation: How College Leaders and Faculty See the Key Issues Facing Higher Education." Report sponsored by the *Chronicle of Higher Education*, underwritten by Adobe Systems and Pearson.

———. 2014. *MOOC U: Who Is Getting the Most Out of Online Education and Why*. New York: Simon & Schuster.

Selwyn, Neil, and Scott Bulfin. 2014. "The Discursive Construction of MOOCs as Educational Opportunity and Educational Threat." Research report from the MOOC Research Institute. www.moocresearch.com.

Siemens, George. 2004. "Connectivism: A Learning Theory for the Digital Age." *Elearnspace* (12 December). www.elearnspace.org/Articles/connectivism.htm.

——. 2013. "Massive Open Online Courses: Innovation in Education?" In *Perspectives on Open and Distance Learning: Open Educational Resources: Innovation, Research and Practice*, edited by Rory McGreal, Wanjira Kinuthia, and Stewart Marshall, 5–15. Athabasca, Canada: Commonwealth of Learning, Athabasca University.

Slaughter, Sheila, and Gary Rhoades. 2004. *Academic Capitalism and the New Economy: Markets, State and Higher Education*. Baltimore: Johns Hopkins University Press.

Slocum, Jenée, and Robert A. Rhoads. 2009. "Faculty and Student Engagement in the Argentine Grassroots Rebellion: Toward a Democratic and Emancipatory Vision of the University." *Higher Education* 57(1): 85–105.

Snow, C. P. 1959. *The Two Cultures and the Scientific Revolution*. Cambridge: Cambridge University Press.

Stewart, Bonnie. 2013. "Not a Hand Up." *Inside Higher Ed* (5 May). www.insidehighered.com.

Stommel, Jesse. 2012. "The March of the MOOCs: Monstrous Open Online Courses." *Hybrid Pedagogy* (23 July). www.hybridpedagogy.com.

Thrun, Sebastian. 2012. "Democratizing Higher Education." Keynote address at the 18th Annual Sloan Consortium International Conference on Online Learning, Lake Buena Vista, Florida, October 10–12.

Tierney, William G., and Guilbert C. Hentschke. 2007. *New Players, Different Game: Understanding the Rise of For-Profit Colleges and Universities*. Baltimore: Johns Hopkins University Press.

Toven-Lindsey, Brit, Robert A. Rhoads, and Jennifer Berdan Lozano. 2015. "Virtually Unlimited Classrooms: Pedagogical Practices in Massive Open Online Courses." *Internet and Higher Education* 24: 1–12.

Tredinnick, Luke. 2006. "Web 2.0 and Business: A Pointer to the Intranets of the Future?" *Business Information Review* 23(4): 228–234.

Turkle, Sherry. 1995. *Life on the Screen: Identity in the Age of the Internet*. New York: Touchstone.

——. 2009. *Simulation and Its Discontents*. Cambridge, MA: MIT Press.

——. 2011. *Alone Together: Why We Expect More from Technology and Less from Each Other*. New York: Basic Books.

UNESCO. 2000. *The Right to Education: Towards Education for All throughout Life*. World Education Report. Paris: UNESCO Publishing.

U.S. Department of Education. 2014. "Enrollment in Distance Education Courses, by State: Fall 2012." Washington, DC: National Center for Education Statistics.

U.S. Senate Committee on Health, Education, Labor, and Pensions (HELP). 2012. "For Profit Higher Education: The Failure to Safeguard the Federal Investment and Ensure Student Success." Official Report from the U.S. Senate (30 July), Washington, DC.

Valls, Andrew. 2013. "Who's Afraid of the Big Bad MOOC?" *Chronicle of Higher Education* (6 May). http://chronicle.com.

Vedder, Richard. 2011. "University of Texas Faculty Workloads Vary Widely." *Austin American Statesman* (4 June). www.statesman.com.

von Hippel, Eric, and Georg von Krogh. 2003. "Open Source Software and the 'Private-Collective' Innovation Model: Issues for Organization Science." *Organization Science* 14(2): 209–223.

Walsh, Taylor. 2011. *Unlocking the Gates: How and Why Leading Universities Are Opening Up Access to Their Courses*. Princeton, NJ: Princeton University Press.

Wang, Yuan, and Ryan Baker. 2014. "MOOC Learner Motivation and Course Completion Rates." Research report from the MOOC Research Institute. www.moocresearch .com.

Warschauer, Mark. 2014. "Peer Assessment and Academic Achievement in a Gateway MOOC." Research report from the MOOC Research Institute. www.moocresearch .com.

Watters, Audrey. 2012. "Confessions of a MOOC-her." *Campus Technology* 26(4): 6.

———. 2013a. "A Future with Only 10 Universities." *Hack Education* (15 October). http:// hackeducation.com.

———. 2013b. "MOOC Mania: Debunking the Hype around Massive Open Online Courses." *The Digital Shift* (18 April). www.thedigitalshift.com.

West, Cornel. 1993. "Preface." In *Paulo Freire: A Critical Encounter*, edited by Peter Leonard and Peter McLaren, xiii–xiv. London: Routledge.

Whitmer, John. 2014. "Patterns of Persistence: What Engages Students in a Remedial English Writing MOOC?" Research report from the MOOC Research Institute. www.moocresearch.com.

Wiley, David. 2013. "What's the Difference between OCWs and MOOCs? Managing Expectations." *Iterating toward Openness* (20 August). http://opencontent.org/blog /archives/2909.

Willinsky, John. 2006. *The Access Principle: The Case for Open Access to Research and Scholarship*. Cambridge, MA: MIT Press.

Wolfman-Arent, Ari. 2014. "Google Will Finance Carnegie Mellon's MOOC Research." *Chronicle of Higher Education* (24 June). http://chronicle.com.

Xu, Di, and Shanna S. Jaggars. 2014. "Performance Gaps between Online and Face-to-Face Courses: Differences across Types of Students and Academic Subject Areas." *Journal of Higher Education* 85(5): 633–659.

Yeager, Carol, Betty Hurley-Dasgupta, and Catherine A. Bliss. 2013. "cMOOCs and Global Learning: An Authentic Alternative." *Journal of Asynchronous Learning Networks* 17(2): 133–147.

Young, Jeffrey R. 2012. "Gates Foundation Gives $9-Million in Grants to Support 'Breakthrough' Education Models." *Chronicle of Higher Education* (19 June). http://chronicle .com.

———. 2013. *Beyond the MOOC Hype: A Guide to Higher Education's High-Tech Disruption.* Washington, DC: Chronicle of Higher Education.

Index